Derya Özkan (ed.)
Cool Istanbul

Urban Studies

Derya Özkan (ed.)

Cool Istanbul

Urban Enclosures and Resistances

[transcript]

Bibliographic information published by the Deutsche Nationalbibliothek
The Deutsche Nationalbibliothek lists this publication in the Deutsche Nationalbibliografie; detailed bibliographic data are available in the Internet at http://dnb.d-nb.de

© 2015 transcript Verlag, Bielefeld

All rights reserved. No part of this book may be reprinted or reproduced or utilized in any form or by any electronic, mechanical, or other means, now known or hereafter invented, including photocopying and recording, or in any information storage or retrieval system, without permission in writing from the publisher.

Cover layout: Kordula Röckenhaus, Bielefeld
Cover illustration: collage by Konrad Bayer, München 2013;
  figures: Derya Özkan
Proofread by Monica Gonzalez-Marquez
Typeset by Till Schmidt
Printed by Majuskel Medienproduktion GmbH, Wetzlar
Print-ISBN 978-3-8376-2763-3
PDF-ISBN 978-3-8394-2763-7

Table of Contents

Cool Istanbul—Urban Enclosures and Resistances
Preface
Derya Özkan | 7

PART I: COOLNESS, VALUE, LABOR

From the Black Atlantic to Cool Istanbul
Why does Coolness matter?
Derya Özkan | 13

The Value of Art and the Political Economy of Cool
Aras Özgün | 35

Reflections on the Panel "Working Poor or Working Deprived in Cool Istanbul?"
An Attempt at Collective Thought
Aslı Odman | 61

PART II: VISUAL IMAGINATIONS OF COOL ISTANBUL

From Wim Wender's Lisbon to Fatih Akın's Istanbul
Producing the Cool City in Film
Özlem Köksal | 81

The City in Black-and-White
Photographic Memories
İpek Türeli | 103

Mirror Mirror on the Wall, Aysel is the Coolest of Them All ...
The Female Protagonist and the Television Series *Kayıp Şehir*
Berrin Yanıkkaya | 131

Index | 163
List of Authors | 171

Cool Istanbul—
Urban Enclosures and Resistances
Preface

DERYA ÖZKAN

This volume is based on a conference that took place November 7-8, 2013, at SALT Galata in Istanbul. The conference was organized in relation to the research project "Changing Imaginations of Istanbul. From Oriental to the Cool City." This currently ongoing project is funded by the DFG's[1] Emmy Noether Program, and hosted by the Institute of European Ethnology at Ludwig Maximilian University of Munich.

The book is composed of two parts. Part I focuses on coolness in relation to value and labor. In Chapter 1, I lay out the coordinates for the discussion on the genealogy of the rubric cool Istanbul. I discuss it in relation to earlier imaginations of the city, to the production of space in the post-fordist metropolis, and last but not the least, to the history of the concept of cool. In Chapter 2, Aras Özgün explores the concept of cool from the perspective of political economy. Comparing it with Immanuel's Kant's conception of the sublime as an aesthetic category that transcends normative beauty, Özgün explores the ways in which cool functions as a substitute for the sublime in the contemporary global culture industry. Özgün draws on the use and exchange value of cool in the context of the post-fordist subjugation of difference to capitalist economy as a source of value. Özgün

[1] DFG or Deutsche Forschungsgemeinschaft is the German Research Foundation.

contextualizes his discussion by referring to Michel Foucault's analysis of the rise of neoliberal governmentality, and the consequences of that in refashioning the privileged status of cultural and artistic production.

Chapter 3 focuses on labor in cool Istanbul, and is the outcome of the two conference panels we initially called "Working Cool Working Poor." Aslı Odman's chapter is based on the narratives by Ayşe Berna Uçarol, Burcu Barakacı, Duygu Semiz, Fikriye Akgül, Melis Tantan, Mustafa Adnan Akyol, Zeycan Elarslan, as well as Odman herself. All are residents of, and workers in, Istanbul. The chapter discusses the impact of the labor regimes in the city on the lives of worker subjects. With an emphasis on how bodies suffer from work, Odman synthesizes the eight workers' accounts in order to compare the working conditions and subjectivities of white and blue collar workers, and as a means to identifying their possible commonalities and differences.

Part II is devoted to analyses of visual imaginations of cool Istanbul. In Chapter 4, Özlem Köksal offers an analysis of how the cool city is produced in film by comparing Fatih Akın's *Crossing the Bridge* with Wim Wender's *Lisbon Story*. Köksal explores the different ways these two films were used to market each respective city, regardless of the intentions of their directors. Köksal's analysis of city films is followed by İpek Türeli's discussion on Ara Güler's black-and-white photographs of Istanbul from the 1950s. In Chapter 5, Türeli investigates how media generated memories of a city's past are used to produce collective understandings of the present. The aesthetics of black-and-white photography as a representational mode, its valorization for producing nostalgia, its reception and appropriation in the form of "monochrome memories," are the foci of Türeli's investigation. Türeli delineates the ways Güler's black-and-white photographs of Istanbul have been instrumental not only in reconstructing the city's past, but also in imagining its future.

Finally, Berrin Yanıkkaya's chapter focuses on the coolness of a female protagonist in a television series. In Chapter 6, Yanıkkaya explains how the representation of Istanbul in *The Lost City* parallels that of the representation of the female character Aysel as complex and multilayered. By referring to feminist literature on the representation of women in visual media, Yanıkkaya shows how the female character Aysel challenges the repertoire of stereotypical female characters in popular media. Yanıkkaya argues that

Aysel embodies the ultimate cool female, as someone who resists hegemonic narratives about sex work, poverty, and *otherness* in the city.

*

The realization of this conference and the publication of this book would not have been possible without the time and effort of the following persons. Above all, I would like to thank the members of the DFG Emmy Noether research group, Aslı Duru, Till Schmidt, Vildan Seçkiner and Yeliz Soytemel for their diligent work in organizing the workshop, and for their continued support and collaboration while preparing this book for publication. Meriç Öner and Deniz Tezucan from SALT made the conference organization flawless with their input as engaged facilitators. I also would like to thank all the other staff members of SALT Galata, not only for lending a helping hand whenever we had a problem, but also for attending the conference sessions entitled "Working Cool Working Poor."

Special thanks go to Till Schmidt for assisting me in editing this book with his patience and precision. Together we had to make hard decisions at multiple turning points, always working against the clock. We had to face the challenge of deadlines, to mediate between the publisher and the authors, to spend hours thinking how to deal with last-minute dropouts. Thanks also to Monica Gonzalez-Marquez, our proofreader, for her careful work. Last but not the least, my warm thanks go to the authors of this book, who meticulously collaborated with us in editing the chapters.

I very much hope that this book will, in some small way, affect its readers' thoughts, ways of seeing and doing, and the ways in which they look at imaginations of Istanbul and other cities.

Derya Özkan, 24 July 2014, Munich

Part I
Coolness, Value, Labor

From the Black Atlantic to Cool Istanbul
Why does Coolness matter?

DERYA ÖZKAN

The departure points for this chapter, as well as for this volume, can be found in my doctoral research.[1] My goal was to try to make sense of Istanbul's everyday spaces, and the ways they were misused by the inhabitants of the city. I focused on the roles people's everyday place-making practices played in the broader production of social space in the city. To understand the political dynamics of misused spaces, I looked closely at the performances of misuse, as well as on the ways these practices were imagined. I found out that they had little legitimacy in the eyes of people at large, and with a media who preferred to speak a socio-normative language about social spaces and life in the city in an effort to conform with the imagined status quo.

The performers were explaining their acts in terms of need and categorizing them as survival strategies. They were themselves not able to conceive of the possibility of misuses being legitimate spatial acts. Normative ideas about what is right and what is wrong were dominating their imagination of their own acts of misuse, and how they made sense of them. Everyday place-making practices also did not receive much affirmation from formally qualified space producers such as architects. Furthermore, govern-

---

1   Özkan, Derya (2008), *"The Misuse Value of Space: Spatial Practices and the Production of Space in Istanbul,"* (Ph.D. diss., University of Rochester). My dissertation is accessible at the following permanent link: http://hdl.-handle.net/1802/6201 (accessed 3 July 2014).

Photograph: Derya Özkan

ing authorities that strived to give order to city spaces, and to keep urban social life under control, interpreted acts of misuse as a threat to the imagined normative urban order.

While inquiring about the imaginations of practices of spatial misuse, I came to understand that there was an emerging reimagining of the city of Istanbul under the rubric "cool Istanbul." Cool Istanbul seemed to be an inclusive body of discourse, giving new value to the older imaginations of the city. It was flexible enough to unite in its own texture the by then outdated characterizations of Istanbul as an oriental city and as a third world city, along with that of a global city.[2] It had a positive rather than a negative, an affirmative rather than a criticizing tone. This suggested a change in discourses on Istanbul, which have long been shaped by the long shadow of global geopolitics. The production of space in Istanbul, as well as that of its imaginations, was inevitably impacted by the hierarchies global power relations have historically affected.

The international edition of *Newsweek* magazine, published the 29th of August, 2005,[3] provided evidence for the argument I was in the process of developing. The cover story read: "Cool Istanbul. Europe's Hippest City. Might Not Need Europe After All."[4] The cover photo is a collage in which two human figures, one male and one female, are dancing, possibly in a nightclub. The female figure is dressed in a way that vaguely suggests belly dancing, presented as an erotic subject, although not stereotypically oriental. The male figure, on the other hand, does not express much masculinity in a "straight" sense; his sexuality makes rather ambiguous erotic suggestions. His shiny satin shirt and pants, along with his necklace, are less masculine than feminine, or suggest at least a new kind of feminized masculinity, or of metro-sexuality, well suited to the imagination of a cool Istanbul that celebrates hybridity as described in the magazine's text.

The *Newsweek* story enabled me to articulate my questions. What does it mean for a city to be cool? What makes Istanbul a cool city? What kinds

---

2   For an overview of this periodization and of how I understand these imaginations, see Özkan, Derya (2012), "Şark Şehrinden 'Cool' Istanbul'a. Değişen Istanbul Tahayyülleri," *Birikim* 277, pp. 76-83.

3   Matthews, Owen and Rana Foroohar (2005), "Turkish delight," *Newsweek* Aug. 29, pp. 31-35.

4   Ibid.

of urban characteristics count as cool in the case of Istanbul? What does that mean in relation to the production of social space in the city in the post-fordist era of neoliberal governmentality in Istanbul? These were the initial questions that eventually led to a new research project intended to investigate what makes cool Istanbul, how and why cool Istanbul, and why now. I wanted to analyze the imaginations of cool Istanbul in relation to the material context in which it was emerging. What did the imagination of cool Istanbul have to do with the materially changing Istanbul increasingly shaped by large-scale urban transformation projects, and by gentrification? What was included in, and excluded from, the imagination of the cool city? What was the politics of this selective inclusiveness, blind to some, yet highly alert to other urban characteristics?

NEGATIVE EARLIER STEREOTYPES, POSITIVE COOL CITY

One of the most salient features of the imagined cool Istanbul was a positive approach, highlighting and celebrating the city's existing urban cultural resources. As the *Newsweek* story outlined, the lure of the city was said to be based on its own "cultural voice growing from within,"[5] the city's rediscovery of its own identity. As the cover emphasized, this identity was not necessarily predominantly European. In other words, Istanbul's coolness did not hinge on the level of Europeanness it had achieved, but on its intrinsic diversity and cosmopolitanism.

This emphasis differed considerably from imaginations of Istanbul as an oriental city, where it was described based on its uncanny difference from European cities. It was also different from Istanbul imagined as a third world city, where it was evaluated in terms of its shortcomings, i.e. inadequate urban infrastructure, qualities that counted as evidence of underdevelopment with respect to European cities. The human, cultural, social resources that the city had been accumulating over thousands of years were positively valued as potential economic capital in the cool city imagination. Currently available yet unexploited resources, the common wealth of the city, were to be celebrated for their power to make a cool Istanbul materialize.

---

5 Ibid.

In this process, freely available cultural features of contemporary urban life that suited to the cool Istanbul imagination were selectively but liberally highlighted and made into objects of fascination. Both materially and immaterially, this helped define the city and shape its new imagination. Among the potentially exploitable resources was also recent urban social history, elements of which were decontextualized and depoliticized in the same process. What I call "gecekondu chic" elsewhere[6] is a very good example of this transformation, in which the history of informal housing in Istanbul was translated into a digestable narrative via mechanisms of objectification, aestheticization and commodification.

Colonialist narratives had defined Istanbul as an oriental city, and developmentalist narratives ascribed to it the geopolitical role of the third world city. The new cool Istanbul imagination opposes while at the same time paradoxically crowns these earlier stereotypes, ways of seeing, and thinking. Seen from the cool Istanbul perspective, neither orientalist nor developmentalist narratives hold any longer: Istanbul does not have to "Europeanize" to be qualified as a cool city. The coolness of Istanbul is still predicated upon the city's "difference;" however, this time "difference" is celebrated as a positive value and not as a lack. Here there is a qualitative change. Difference, along with diversity, is a value of global currency, as in other areas of urban and cultural production in the era of post-fordism. Inclusion overruns exclusion. The embrace of difference comes first, only followed later, when and where it is necessary, by exclusionary strategies to control the population. The emphasis shifts from hegemonic top-down sovereignty to subject-driven governmentality.

For instance, the belly dancer is a figure formerly used to suggest orientalism, yet has been rediscovered as an element of urban cultural heritage worth celebrating, so long as it is integrated into a global vocabulary. It is now common to come across belly dancers as part of experimental music

---

6   A short article based on this work has been published: Özkan, Derya (2014), "Informal settlements and urban poverty as cultural commodity," *dérive*. *Zeitschrift für Stadforschung* 56, pp. 43-46 (also available at: http://www.eurozine.com/articles/2014-07-11-ozkan-en.html, accessed 30 July 2014). For an earlier Turkish version, see Özkan, Derya (2012), "Gecekondu Chic? Kültürel meta olarak enformel şehir ve kent yoksulluğu," *Birikim* 280-281, pp. 155-160.

performances in trendy jazz bars in Istanbul, such as Babylon.[7] When recontextualized, belly dancing no longer suggests a negative sense of orientalism; it becomes one among many "authentic" colors of the city, processed and made into one of the many cultural highlights of a cool Istanbul.

A similar example would be kebabs. When they first began to be integrated in the cuisine of Istanbul, they were not welcome by the city's elite. They were imagined as unwanted, crude elements of 20th century Istanbul and its population. They were imagined as brought by migrants coming from eastern provinces and contaminating the otherwise refined Istanbul cuisine with their impure, un-urbane cultures. Later, kebabs were promoted to the status of a specialist cuisine, produced and consumed in the expensive upper class restaurants of the city. And thus, they were contained and embraced by bourgeois Istanbulites.

In the framework of cool Istanbul, kebab acquires another value that takes it beyond its bourgeois domestication. According to the writers of the Istanbul Eats blog, the distinctive kebab is to be found in the city's "culinary backstreets."[8] That is, if you are looking for good, authentic kebabs, they recommend you go to small, unknown restaurants in shady parts of the city, rather than the upscale chains located in fancy neighborhoods such as Develi in Etiler or Namlı in Levent, places where the urban elite embraced and appropriated the kebab.[9]

This is a new regime of imagination that renders belly dancing, kebab and gecekondu cool by placing them in new contexts. These urban cultural traits are cool only when they are recontextualized and reframed, not in their conflict-full historical, cultural and political materiality but as reduced to consumable cultural commodities. This process affects immediate images and thoughts in the minds of people, often in ways that never actually

---

7   The Istanbul based band *Baba Zula* has done this multiple times in Babylon. See: http://www.babazula.com/ (accessed 3 July 2014).

8   *Istanbul Eats: A Serious Eaters' Guide to the City* is a blog run by Ansel Mullins and Yigal Schleifer (http://Istanbuleats.com/, accessed 3 July 2014). They have also published a food guidebook with the same title: Mullins, Ansel and Yigal Schleifer (2010), *Istanbul Eats: Exploring the Culinary Backstreets*, Istanbul: Boyut Publishing.

9   Kozanoğlu, Can. (1992), *Cilâlı imaj devri: 1980'lerden 90'lara Türkiye ve starları*, Istanbul: İletişim Yayınları.

touch the bitter and difficult sides of the story, i.e. all the bodily suffering urban poverty brings with it in the case of lives in the *gecekondu*. Examples of this kind of new imaginative framing can also be found in contemporary art, in which *gecekondu* is celebrated for the spontaneous, informal and flexible characteristics of its spatial production. However, the material production of the *gecekondu* is often not touched upon. Artworks featuring or commenting on *gecekondu* mostly positively emphasize what makes the *gecekondu* an exciting piece of space, often for the resourcefulness of its creators. These works do not simultaneously dwell upon the political economy of the *gecekondu* or what in material terms facilitates that spontaneity, informality and flexibility. The question of the social costs incurred to have a *gecekondu* come into being is largely ignored in cases of aestheticized *gecekondu* imaginations.[10]

Another similar example is the recently partially evacuated Tarlabaşı neighborhood, which became cool only at the moment of its destruction. As Begüm Özden Fırat discussed,[11] the evacuated and destroyed social space of the neighborhood, materially the living space of Istanbul's non-Muslim populations in the nineteenth century, and then of poor migrants coming from rural areas in the twentieth, now all evicted for urban redevelopment, became the subject of what Fırat called a "pornographic gaze," as it came to constitute a decorative background to street arts festivals. After the neighborhood Sulukule went through a violent urban transformation and attracted wide international attention, Tarlabaşı became one of the most popular destinations in Istanbul for artists. They not only instrumentalized their art to help resist violent top-down urban transformation projects, but they also used these lived social spaces as stages in which to locate their artistic performances.

Before I move on, let me pose another series of questions: What does this historically specific shift in the imaginations of Istanbul suggest? What does it mean when difference, diversity, imperfection, urban chaos, informality, flexibility and spontaneity of a city are uncritically celebrated? Can we say that cool Istanbul is the post-fordist embrace of the formerly de-

---

10 Özkan (2014), "Informal settlements."
11 Özden Fırat, Begüm (2012), "Tarlabaşı'nda sanat: Yıkıma dek görülebilir!" *Bir+Bir* 18. The text can be retrieved online at: http://birdirbir.org/tarlabasinda-sanat-yikima-dek-gorulebilir/ (accessed 3 July 2014).

nounced qualities of the city? Is cool a paradigm for cultural production in post-fordist urban society? Furthermore, is cool a paradigm for the social production of life in post-fordism? Is it a paradigm for the material production of the post-fordist city, in which cultural production takes on an increasingly more hegemonic role in urban economy?

COOL ISTANBUL—
NEW ENCLOSURES IN THE POST-FORDIST CITY

Before I engage in the questions that I posed above, I would like to clarify how I conceptualize the relationship between the material production of the city's spaces, and the production of their imaginations. The imagination of a city is not subordinate to its material production. That is, it is more than a symptom of something more substantial than itself. Imaginations of cities are socially produced, and this social production is integral to cities' material production. A better way of conceiving this relationship is to see it as a field of constantly changing and back-and-forth moving encounters, exchanges and effects. Not only does the city produce imaginations, imaginations also produce the city.

Who then are the actors of these productions? What roles do they play in producing the city and in producing its imaginations? *Newsweek* highlighted that the coolness of Istanbul was produced from within, and not imposed from without. *Newsweek* makes it clear that Istanbul's coolness originates from its own culture. Istanbul is said to have the power to rediscover its voice and revitalize it. It is worth noting that the metaphor used here for culture, namely "the cultural voice growing from within," is an organic one. It is meant to conceptualize the city as a body that recreates itself anew. It is as if an organic entity were in the process of "becoming."[12]

---

12 "Becoming" has been used as a qualifier for Istanbul and other places frequently within the last ten years. One reason might be the popularization of the idea of spaces and places as constantly changing social formations. In the case of Istanbul, there were two significant exhibitions of this sort: *"Becoming a Place,"* 2001, Proje 4L, Istanbul, and *"Becoming Istanbul,"* 2008, DAM, Frankfurt (Main). A book was published for the former exhibition: Açıkkol, Özge (Ed.) (2001), *Becoming a Place/Yerleşmek*, Istanbul: Proje 4L-Istanbul

Istanbul in this period becomes a city defined with respect to notions of incompletion and imperfection,[13] all seen in a positive light. What is so special here about the becoming status of Istanbul?

In relation to both the human subject and the city, coolness can be thought of as self-fashioning. The self in a post-fordist regime of government is constantly becoming. The established order of things demands that the subject continuously make and improve itself, make the best of human capital, be productive and efficient in a way that is less stable than dynamic. Post-fordism demands a high level of self-confidence from its subjects. This regime requires its subjects to catch up with the constantly changing and simultaneously expanding requirements of post-fordist social production. Selves are life projects.[14] One is forced to become an entrepreneur of oneself. In this sense, I ask, is cool the social ontology of post-fordism?

In the case of cool Istanbul, cool is a paradigm for urban cultural production, one that is marked by non-conformity, resistance to the mainstream, dissent and risk. Cool cultural production strives for superiority

---

Museum of Contemporary Art. The latter was originally a project by the Garanti Gallery, exhibited later in 2011 at SALT Beyoğlu, Istanbul, and then translocated to the web as a database accessible online: http://database.becomingIstanbul.org/ (accessed 18 June 2014). A book was also published accompanying the *Becoming Istanbul* exhibition: Derviş, Pelin; Tanju, Bülent and Uğur Tanyeli (Ed.s) (2008), *Becoming Istanbul. An Encyclopedia*, Istanbul: Garanti Gallery.

13 "Imperfection" was the theme of the first Istanbul Design Biennial in 2012, proposed by Deyan Sudjic, a member of the Biennial advisory board, and director of the Design Museum, London. See: http://Istanbuldesignbiennial.iksv.org/about/biennial-theme/ (accessed 18 June 2014). Another example that fits this trend was an exhibition entitled "Ability to face the uncertain," which was a collaborative project that took place in the form of several exhibitions along Serdar-ı Ekrem Caddesi in Galata from 5 to 15 July 2010. For the poster of the exhibition, which is worth seeing, go to: http://v3.arkitera.com/e3561-belirsizlikleri-gogusleyebilme-becerisi.html (accessed 18 June 2014).

14 See the cover of the magazine *Spiegel Wissen*, the title of which is "Projekt: Ich. Neue Strategien für ein besseres Leben" (Project: I. New strategies for a better life): http://www.spiegel.de/spiegel/spiegelwissen/index-2013-3.html (accessed 18 June 2014).

over mainstream cultural production by capitalizing on differences rather than evening them out, by successful risk-taking. In this sense, I ask, is coolness a new paradigm for aesthetic judgment in post-fordism? Is it perhaps a new sublime?[15]

The cool may also be considered as a paradigm for the post-fordist production of social life. In the case of the cool city, it is social life in the city that makes it cool. In the case of Istanbul, this takes the form of embracing the anomalous elements of that life. It is a transformative enfolding of the once risky and challenging urban elements (people, places, etc.) that were formerly considered almost not worth caring for, or stigmatized for being irregular and deviant with regard to desired urban social norms.

The Tarlabaşı neighborhood mentioned earlier is a case in point. Before the cool hype set in, the neighborhood was for a long time seen as a no-go area, where Roma and Kurdish immigrant communities lived together, although not necessarily without conflict. It was declared a declining neighborhood with poor physical and social living conditions. Tarlabaşı was associated with crime, drugs, etc., and stigmatized as a dangerous area.

Once enclosed by the cool city imagination, Tarlabaşı became a cool place to use as a background for street arts festivals, a popular hang-out for Erasmus students, inspiration for artists, an urban field to learn from for researchers, and a place of engagement for urban activists. The question is, how and why does a neighborhood, subjected to a violent urban transformation project that evicts poor people from their homes and forces them to move to the outskirts of the city, become a point of attraction, in particular to an educated urban elite, either visiting or living in Istanbul.

In keeping with the Tarlabaşı example, can we understand the cool city as an enclosure of commonly produced urban cultural wealth? What makes cool urban cultures? Isn't it the urban cultural resources and everyday life practices readily available in the city that are enclosed as the cool city? In this sense, isn't the cool city commonly produced urban social life, later branded by city marketing professionals, instrumentalized and deployed to promote the city? Moreover, what happens under conditions of this kind of enclosure? What is the impact of the enclosure of urban cultural common resources on the urban economy, if not to boost it for capitalist profit? Most

---

15 For a discussion of the concept of cool in relation to the concept of the sublime, see the chapter in this volume by Aras Özgün.

importantly, what is the impact of city marketing on the lives of the multitude,[16] exploited and repressed in diverse ways with respect to class, gender and race?

To find clues to answer these questions, or rather, to refine and sharpen these questions, and to highlight their urgency, Aslı Duru[17] and I led a series of focus group discussions in the "beautiful summer" of 2013 in Istanbul -- marked by the remarkably cool Gezi resistance. Our major aim was to understand what people living in the city associated with cool Istanbul, what cool Istanbul meant to them, whether or not it meant anything at all. We asked them questions about what they considered cool urban spatial practices in Istanbul.[18]

I would like to emphasize here an important research shift our focus group discussions with the inhabitants of Istanbul affected. This was an irrevocable shift of focus from consumption-based to use-based accounts, related to needs and desires. Although focus group participants also reproduced the commercial and consumption-based *Newsweek*-like discourses at times, there was a clear need and a strongly use-related desire for cool spaces and practices. The participants' focus was very realistic: it was more centered on accessible, rehabilitating practices than abstract and intangible ones.

In summary, the point of departure for thinking was less immaterial than material for them. It was about a need to rehabilitate from the ills of a city shaped by neoliberal urban policies that were increasingly restricting the urban inhabitants' lives, and narrowing down their lifeworlds. They could not move easily in the city, go from one place to the other without spending hours in traffic, for instance. It was a desire to open up that lifeworld to accessible, affordable yet pleasurable experiences. For the focus group participants, everyday/ordinary escapes from the constraints imposed

---

16   Hardt, Michael and Antonio Negri (2004), *Multitude: War and Democracy in the Age of Empire*, New York: The Penguin Press.

17   Aslı Duru has been a Postdoctoral Research Fellow since 2012 in the DFG Emmy Noether research project that led to this volume.

18   I am currently working on an article tentatively entitled "Cool Istanbul: City as Common Wealth, Space of Entrapment and Rehabilitation." In this text, I analyze our focus group findings in detail.

upon their lives by the political economy of the cool city counted as cool practices.

It is in this sense that I would like to reclaim cool spaces and practices in the city and discuss them in relation to the concept of everyday resistance. I refer to acts of passive resistance in everyday life, practices that are neither necessarily nor explicitly intended as resistance. It involves moments of taking a silent yet non-conformist stand in everyday situations, inventing ways to deal with repressive conditions. It is not so much about fighting it out as it is about disobedience and refusal to conform to acts of enclosure.[19] It may be relatively invisible to the eyes of an onlooker, whereas it might be vital to those who create ways of living within the given social landscape. Cool resistance operates at the level of small gestures, instead of grand, ground-breaking acts. It is not a comprehensive social revolution. Rather, it is geared towards creating tiny little singular cracks in the status quo, sometimes only on the surface, others going through capillary vessels deep into the flesh of the urban fabric.

THE GENEALOGY OF THE CONCEPT OF COOL

The cool attitude has to do with maintaining dignity. It is a protective shield covering the self momentarily against the repressive blows of social life. The subject secures itself with coolness as a weapon against all that in social life which would threaten the self's composure. Performing a cool attitude is a constant fight not to lose composure as a subject. Coolness

---

19   The non-conformism I discuss here is akin to what Asef Bayat defines as "the silent encroachment of the ordinary" in his studies on poor people's tactics of everyday resistance in Iran. See Bayat, Asef (1997), *Street Politics: Poor People's Movements in Iran*, New York: Columbia University Press; Bayat (1997), "Un-Civil Society: The Politics of the Informal People," *Third World Quarterly* 18 (1), pp. 53-72; Bayat (2010), *Life as Politics. How Ordinary People Change the Middle East*, Amsterdam: Amsterdam University Press. Also relevant to this discussion are the following: Scott, James (1987), *Weapons of the Weak. Everyday Forms of Peasant Resistance*, Yale University Press; and de Certeau, Michel (1984), *The Practice of Everyday Life,* Berkeley: University of California Press.

means a calm audaciousness, a state of keeping one's fearlessness under control for the sake of dignified survival. It is not at all a coincidence that there are idioms in the English language such as "keep one's cool" (keep one's nerves under control, stay calm), "lose one's cool" (lose one's temper, become suddenly angry) "to blow one's cool" (lose one's composure, to become frantic).[20]

The etymology of the word cool takes us to the history of the Atlantic slave trade, to "the black Atlantic."[21] In his studies of African art, Robert Farris Thompson traced the origins of the word to Africa, where it has been used in thirty five languages, as an all-emcompasing positive attribute combining composure, silence, vitality, healing and social purification, as a basic metaphor of moral aesthetic accomplishment.[22] According to Thompson, the concept of cool stands somewhere between the sacred and the profane in African cultures, being transferred from there to America during the slave trade chapter in capitalism, and thus acquiring its modern meanings.[23]

Thompson analyzes the meanings of coolness in African languages and cultures, as well as in African art, in extensive detail. He emphasizes that it refers to a high degree of self-control, a moderation in coldness, calmness in times of stress. A West African definition is "to reveal no emotion in situations where excitement and sentimentality are acceptable, to act as though one's mind were in another world."[24] It involves fulfilling difficult

---

20 Merriam-Webster online dictionary (www.merriam-webster.com). See also the entries in the online Etymology Dictionary (http://www.etymonline.com/) and Urban Dictionary (www.urbandictionary.com). (accessed 3 July 2014)

21 Gilroy, Paul (1993), *The Black Atlantic: Modernity and Double Consciousness*, Cambridge: Harvard University Press.

22 Thompson, Robert Farris (1973), "An Aesthetic of the Cool," *African Art* 7 (1), pp. 41-91. Thompson's writings on the concept of cool were compiled and (re)published in one volume in 2011: Thompson, Robert Farris, *Aesthetic of the Cool. Afro-Atlantic Art and Music*, New York City: Periscope Publishing. In his book *Cool Capitalism*, Jim McGuigan draws on Thompson's study from the 1970s (2009, London: Pluto Press: p.1).

23 An analysis of the modern history of cool can be found in: Pountain, Dick and David Robins (2000), *Cool Rules: Anatomy of an Attitude*, London: Reaktion.

24 Thompson (1973), "An Aesthetic of the Cool," p.16-17.

tasks with an air of ease and silent disdain. In other words, can we say that coolness means prefering the unacceptable to the acceptable? Does it imply a kind of non-conformism? A silent non-conformity that despises the situation and keeps calmly thinking that "another world is possible"?

Thompson continues to explain that the mask of coolness is worn not only in times of stress but also of pleasure. "Cooling one's heart" helps achieve the restoration of tranquility. African definitions of mystical or metaphorical "coolness" involve discretion, healing, rebirth and purity, but they are not necessarily similar to Western notions of icy determination.[25] Coolness ceases pain, brings serenity. Being cool makes one as placid "as the surface of the water."[26] The terms "cool mouth" (*enun tutu*) in Yoruba language and "cool tongue" (*kanua kahoro*) in Kikuyu language both suggest an intelligent withholding of speech for the purpose of higher deliberation. Coolness in this sense functions as "the mask of the mind."[27]

Thompson shows, in his analysis of African figural sculpture, that coolness involves not only the mind but instead a body that includes the mind, blending its muscular force with mental respectability, demonstrating one's bold character, rendering the physical body politically powerful.[28] He traces the genealogy of the concept of cool to the sculpted heads of kings and gods from the ninth to the fifteenth centuries. In those faces marked by serenity, "certainty and calm from the past is transferred to the present as a phenomenon of mirrored order;" they reflect a transition "from this world to the next."[29]

Despite appearing ahistorical or too speculative, the mystical side of African "coolness" is reminiscent of *Newsweek's* imagination of cool Istanbul, whose coolness emerges from its own "cultural voice growing from within," or from the city's rediscovery of its own identity. Just as African sculpted heads of kings and gods are supposed to represent continuity with the past, Istanbul's coolness is thought to originate in its very own cultural accumulation over centuries, from the power and self-confidence the ex-imperial city regains to rediscover its own resources and become revital-

---

25 Ibid.
26 Ibid, p.18.
27 Ibid.
28 Ibid.
29 Ibid, p.19.

ized. The mysticism of ninth to fifteenth century African culture finds a peculiar counterpart in the post-fordist mystification of a city's economic and cultural revitalization.

Another similar characteristic of Western African mystic coolness and Istanbul's coolness as a city can be found in the emphasis on the claim that coolness cannot be inherited but can only be achieved. The social ontology of Western African culture, as explained by Thompson, is strikingly similar to that of the contemporary subject in the case of cool Istanbul, a reminder of the post-fordist embrace of cultural capital, as discussed above in terms of the self-fashioning of the human subject. The self in West African culture, as well as in post-fordist regime of government, has to make the best of its past and activate its human capital. It has to fashion itself to catch up with the constantly changing and simultaneously expanding requirements of social life.

In the context of the Atlantic slave trade, coolness was the description of an attitude of silent contempt, a resentful silence, that slaves used in the face of enslavement and their inability to rise against it, as the cost of protest would have been too high. It is in this sense that the cool attitude corresponds to resistance, to the ability to stay calm and dignified under conditions of repression. Coolness then helps to reinforce subjects striving to remain unperturbed by the consequences of restrictive social conditions, or the repressive city. Coolness enables the subject to overcome the sorrow created by repression. Coolness indicates not only the ability to produce an affect but also the power to be affected, and more importantly, to deal with affect. In this sense, it is not only healing but also empowering and liberating, as it moves one towards joy.[30]

When looking into the history of popular culture in the twentieth century, one can put a finger on the changing meanings of cool. The history of African-American jazz music and culture[31] follows the Atlantic slave trade

---

30 This formulation is inspired by Spinoza, who describes how the body acquires joy, and how this empowers the body once it is affected by something that affirms it. See Deleuze, Gilles (2006 [1978]), *Spinoza Üzerine Onbir Ders*, translated and compiled by Ulus Baker, Istanbul: Kabalcı Yayınevi.

31 I am completing this text in my office at Oettingenstrasse 67, in a building located near the English Garden in Munich. Now hosting several institutes of Ludwig Maximilian University of Munich, this building was used *by Radio*

as a context for coolness in the United States. Cool was part of the slang language used by rebellious bebop musicians, and was later taken up by the dominant white culture and integrated into popular everyday language in the US. In the essay entitled "The White Negro. Superficial Reflections on the Hipster," Norman Mailer wrote about young white people in the 1920s, 30s and 40s in the US, who liked jazz music and adopted black culture.[32] For Mailer, cool was an attribute of the hipster.

I agree with Dick Pountain and David Robins that, compared to hipster, cool is a concept that has a grasp on a wider landscape of affect and a longer history, and that it could also be attributed to objects, not just people.[33] In *Cool Rules. Anatomy of an Attitude*, Pountain and Robins show how the cool attitude, which originally expressed resistance to subjugation, was first transformed into a new kind of passive resistance to the work ethic through personal style, then expropriated by the mass media and advertising industries of the 1980s and 90s, and used to seduce young consumers. Pountain

---

Free Europe after the Second World War. Beginning in 1951, many well-known African-American jazz artists, such as Ella Fitzgerald, Louis Armstrong, and Dizzy Gillespie were guests in radio programs. Radio Free Europe, founded by the US state department and monitored by the CIA, aimed to fight communism by broadcasting news and features from Munich to countries behind the Iron Curtain during the Cold war. RFE used the building on Oettingenstrasse in Munich until 1995, when its headquarters was moved to Prague. This is just a short note on how this concrete place connects to what I am writing about. For more on Radio Free Europe, see Radio Free Europe/Radio Liberty website: http://www.rferl.org/info/history/133.html (accessed 3 July 2014). The archive of the radio is today located at the Hoover Institution Archives at Stanford University: http://www.hoover.org/library-archives (accessed 3 July 2014). There is an ongoing archival project in which the archival material is digitized and made available to researchers: Radio Free Europe Project: http://hoorferl.stanford.edu/RFE/index.php (accessed 3 July 2014). See also the website of the experimental project Radio Free Europe Reloaded, realized in situ in 2013/4 at Oettingenstrasse. (http://rferl.info/, accessed 3 July 2014).

32 See Mailer, Norman (1957), "The White Negro. Superficial Reflections on the Hipster," *Dissent. A Quarterly of Politics and Culture* (Fall).
33 Pountain and Robins (2000): *Cool rules*, p.41.

and Robbins identify three major characteristics of the contemporary cool attitude, namely narcissism, ironic detachment and hedonism.[34] Ironic detachment was a major element of the cool attitude of the black slave, making it possible for her to maintain a protective cool persona.[35] Hedonism appeared as a distinctive characteristic reflecting one's own gratification. The hippies in particular, and the 1960s countercultures and dissident social movements in general, strived to liberate themselves from the ills of mass society through the power of hedonism. Narcissism, on the other hand, functioned as a healthy celebration of the self.

As Thomas Frank outlines in *The Conquest of Cool*, the cool oppositional youth cultures of the 1960s were co-opted by the mainstream cultures of the 1990s, creating a cool attitude politically domesticated and contained by capitalism.[36] Frank analyzes the ways in which the rebellious elements in the 1960s social movements were translated into one of the major building blocks of business culture in the United States in the 1990s, how corporations revolutionized their management practices by making (mis)use of and normalizing rebel ideologies. This manifested as a rejection of the 1950s status quo, exemplified by mass production and consumption, thus paving the way for non-conformity to become one of the major elements of mainstream culture. The cool of the 1990s is thus the non-conformist, narcissistic subject of corporate business, which would later find expression in the post-fordist subject, culture and aesthetics.

In his book *Cool Capitalism*, Jim McGuigan dwells on the role of cool in translating disaffection into acceptance and compliance, and thus in helping to legitimize capitalism.[37] In McGuigan's terminology, cool capitalism is "the marriage of counter-culture and corporate business."[38] In other words, capitalism responds to criticism by stealing the weapons of those who oppose it; it incorporates dissent into its own institutions. On the other hand, Ulla Haselstein and Irmela Hijiya-Kirschnereit define cool as a

---

34 Ibid.
35 Ibid, p.27.
36 Frank, Thomas (1997), *The Conquest of Cool:Business Culture, Counterculture, and the Rise of Hip Consumerism*. Chicago: University of Chicago Press.
37 McGuigan (2009), *Cool Capitalism*.
38 Ibid, p. 7.

metaphorical term for affect control.[39] Emphasizing that there are distinct cultural traditions of affect control, Haselstein and Hijiya-Kirschnereit dwell on the gendered, ethnicized instances of the cool in America and Japan, as well as explore the Stoic and Roman, "antique" cools. Richard Majors and Janet Mancini also explore the cool from the perspective of ethnicity and gender in their book *Cool Pose: The Dilemmas of Black Manhood in America*, discussing its predominantly male character in African-American cultures.[40] Peter Stearns, on the other hand, studies coolness as part of his larger project "The History of the Emotions in America" in his *American Cool: Constructing a Twentieth-Century Emotional Style*, and argues that coolness in the 20th century replaced 19th century sentimentalism.[41]

I take the cool attitude as both an expression of a desire for liberation, and an attempt to produce distinction despite (or in response to) repression.[42] In other words, taking up coolness is a silent expression of the desire for liberation, by means of which the subject is produced. Coolness is an integral part of the formation of the subject that immanently resists repression. I understand distinction as more ontological than sociological. Distinction makes sense to me only in relation to the social production of the

---

39 Haselstein, Ulla and Imela Hijiya-Kirschnereit (2013), "Introduction," in *The Cultural Career of Coolness. Discourses and Practices of Affect Control in European Antiquity, the United States, and Japan*, ed. Ulla Haselstein et al., New York: Lexington Books.

40 Majors, Richard and Janet Mancini Billson (1992), *Cool Pose: The Dilemmas of Black Manhood in America*, New York: Lexington Books.

41 Stearns, Peter N. (1994), *American Cool Constructing a Twentieth Century Emotional Style*, New York: New York University Press.

42 The concept of distinction I use here refers to Bourdieu, although I also criticize his interpretation of this concept. Bourdieu takes distinction to belong exclusively to and be produced by the upper classes. Bourdieu's approach is blind to the versions of distinction produced elsewhere by other people, by other means, and in not so easily predictable ways. Jacques Ranciere develops a good criticism of Bourdieu's concept of distinction. See Bourdieu, Pierre (1984), *Distinction: A SocialCcritique of the Judgement of Taste*, Cambridge, Mass: Harvard University Press; Rancière, Jacques (2004), *The Philosopher and His Poor*, Durham, NC: Duke University Press.

subject, or to *le dispositif* as Foucault theorizes it, that is, not only as a habitus-carrying being but also as a potentially habitus-challenging becoming.[43]

The cool attitude, then, has to do with the habitus from which the subject is molded; however, the same subject also has the capacity to mold that habitus into something beyond it, to the extent that the habitus becomes unrecognizable, from one moment to the other, in a flash, as Walter Benjamin would describe it. For Benjamin, the dialectical relation between the past and the present is not that one casts its light on the other. For him, it is the constellation formed "wherein what has been comes together in a flash with the now" that points to a revolutionary moment in history.[44] The way I understand the moment the subject takes on a cool attitude is similar to the flash that Benjamin describes.

It is in this sense that I would like to rethink and reclaim the concept of cool with an emphasis on the body's capacity to become and to overcome. This is not necessarily in the form of a resistance that poses itself against the establishment and fights against it, nor in the form of an opposition to the mainstream aspects of social life for the sake of sociological distinction. It does not necessarily generate material or immaterial currency. It is neither an activist's resistance nor the rebellious popular cultures of the 1990s. I am talking instead about a politicized and embodied meaning of the cool. I propose a change in the way we see the resistance act in keeping cool, not in the direction of ressentiment but in the form of a constantly becoming life-affirming bodily practice.

---

43   Bourdieu takes habitus as an overwhelming determinant of the social being, while disregarding the subject-driven disturbances that constantly threaten its consistency (see: Bourdieu, Pierre [1977], *Outline of a Theory of Practice*, New York: Cambridge University Press). The line of Foucauldian-Deleuzian thinking offers useful tools to developing criticisms of Bourdieu's concept of habitus. See the 1977 interview with Foucault: "The Confession of the Flesh," in *Space, Knowledge and Power Foucault and Geography*, ed. Jeremy W. Crampton and Stuart Elden, Aldershot: Ashgate.

44   Benjamin, Walter (1999), *The Arcades Project*, Cambridge, Mass: Belknap Press, p. 463.

COOL GEZI

Gezi resistance in Istanbul in the summer of 2013 was a remarkable example of the kind of politicized and embodied coolness I talk about. Contrary to accounts that declared that Gezi was the end of cool Istanbul, I argue that Gezi was exceedingly cool.[45] On the 1st of June, 2013, masses of people flowed through the Bosporus bridge from the Asian to the European side of Istanbul. The same evening, the first public gathering in Munich in support of the Gezi resistance took place at Odeonsplatz. I went to this meeting carrying a hand-made corrugated cardboard sign that read "this is cool Istanbul." Not much attention was paid to my sign in that politically agitated atmosphere, but in the following days and weeks I was frequently asked what had happened to "my cool Istanbul." My answer was "cool Istanbul exploded."

It was the resistance immanent in the social bodies that made Gezi cool. In other words, in the Gezi resistance, cool Istanbul was produced inside and from below, through a lived and living coolness on the ground. Gezi moved coolness beyond mainstream commercial accounts of cool Istanbul, the images produced by international media and catered to tourists. Cool Istanbul found its material form in the social body made up of the bodies of the multitude in Gezi Park, where it was so cool not to have to pay for anything that one needed, from water to cigarettes to food.

Gezi resistance produced extremely creative and powerful images in a very short time. Images of people with gas masks, of bodies confronting police shields immediately became iconized locally, and popularized globally, mainly thanks to their extensive circulation in social media. Not surprisingly, this imagery could not escape immediate enclosures. Gas masks became cool. Symbols of the Gezi resistance were quickly included in the cool Istanbul imagination.[46]

---

45 Mutlu, Yetkin (2014), "The end of Cool Istanbul," *Qantara*, 31 January 2014: http://en.qantara.de/content/culture-in-turkey-before-and-after-gezi-the-end-of-cool-Istanbul (accessed 24 June 2014).

46 An example of this (from below) is the following blog entry: Ciarmello, Christine, "Cool Istanbul and my Tear Gas hangover" (http://www.cciarm.com/random-rantings/Istanbul-smells-like-tear-gas, accessed 24 June 2014).

In the case of Gezi, via the creative production of social life, images, ideas, humor, and most importantly of resistance, we had an affirmative political moment in which the cool took on new meanings, more complicated than those intended predominantly for capitalist profit and/or conformist ends, forms that had been already covered extensively by *Newsweek* and similar outlets. The Gezi resistance shook and disturbed everything it touched, including our research project. As the members of a research group working on Istanbul, we began to rethink the framework in which we had been discussing the concept of cool in relation to the city of Istanbul. It changed our research foci and directions. "Çapulcuyuz ama havamız yerinde" (we are looters but we are cool) was one of the unforgettable mottos that characterized the coolness of the Gezi park occupation and its creators.[47]

EVERYDAY COOL, LIFE ITSELF

A cool political explosion like Gezi does not happen every day. However, practices of cool resistance are abundant everywhere, at any time. This is not to idealize coolness or resistance but to suggest looking at cool Istanbul from the perspective of material, embodied, everyday resistance. There is no guarantee that coolness will always turn into a liberating resistance. There are also ressentiments, negative ontologies, which often do not allow for much creativity. In fact, in the ordinary goings-on of everyday life, there is a lot of room to fall into the trap of moments of ressentiment as a protective shield whenever it isn't possible to mitigate repression materially and/or immaterially. Coolness includes those moments as well. The question is how to develop an awareness of everyday acts, how to transform everyday practices and channel them towards more liberating ones. I am

---

47   During the Gezi protests, prime minister Tayyip Erdoğan used the word "çapulcu" (looter) to denounce the protestors. The term was quickly appropriated by the protestors as an affirmative description of themselves. It was also adopted by other languages, i.e. transformed into "chapulling" in English or "chapullieren" in German, to mean fighting for one's rights. Thanks to Vildan Seçkiner who brought the scarf with the motto "Çapulcuyuz ama havamız yerinde" (we are looters but we are cool) from Istanbul.

very much aware that there is no shortcut answer to this question. I guess it is all in there, in one's own life, in the form of acts, re-acts and counter-acts. I suppose it is in the very gist of life itself.

The Value of Art and the Political Economy of Cool

ARAS ÖZGÜN

Cool is a very vague term in the way we use it in everyday language. It may function as an affirmative verbal cue, i.e. we use it instead of "ok" or "yes" It may function as an exclamation expressing different strengths of affirmation, i.e. "that's cool!" or simply "cool, then..." It expresses subcultural identity in American English, and appears as a code switching device in other languages to inform a familiarity with that subcultural code, and therefore it signals an attitude, a way of life that is characterized by these types of familiarities. On the cover of *Newsweek*,[1] it attributes a particular type of value to a distant cultural signifier—Istanbul—by indiscernably associating it with all these affirmative transitional codes.

As vague and ephemeral as it is, cool appears to be a dominant form of value in contemporary cultural economy and urban culture—as the cover of the *Newsweek* illustrates. Therefore, in my view, a critical discussion of the production and circulation of *cool* can provide us with clues to understanding contemporary capitalist economy in general. This chapter pursues a discussion of the value of *cool* in a political economic context. I will examine its relationship with the global culture industry, post-fordist economic conditions, and neoliberal cultural policies.

I will begin by interrogating the meaning of the term more closely in order to reveal the parallelism it implies with another form of value dis-

---

1   See the chapter by Derya Özkan in this volume for a discussion about the cover of the international edition of *Newsweek* from 2005.

Photograph: Derya Özkan

tinctly related with artistic production (rather than that of ordinary cultural artifacts). Following this lead, and drawing on that parallelism, I discuss how this distinct form of aesthetic value becomes translated into a dominant form of economic value, and then becomes incorporated within postfordist production cycles. I will argue that the urban transformation of Istanbul over the past decades exemplifies this incorporation, and articulates the new economic logic perfectly. Yet, this articulation does not remain uncontested. While referring to a dominant form of value in a new political economic context, I will argue in conclusion that, cool originally affirms a subversive political ethos that continues to challenge the postfordist accumulation regimes, and neoliberal governmentality—as the recent urban uprisings in Istanbul exemplify.

I. COOL & SUBLIME

According to the *New Oxford American Dictionary*, the definition of cool is "fashionably attractive, impressive."[2] This is the fashionable use of the term that barely scratches the surface of the depth of its actual meaning, or the depth of the cultural relations it signifies. However, the common dictionary definition provides us with an entry point to our discussion; it refers to a value judgment that cannot be easily substituted with other positive attributes to signify aesthetic appeal. In the context of popular culture, cool is not beautiful, it's not nice or pretty—it's often times not even good. Fashionable is the key term here, i.e. *fashionably attractive*. Cool signifies a novelty, points to the temporariness of its object. In this sense, cool resembles the notion of the sublime in the context of aesthetics, and as I will argue, it also refers to a similar cultural economy.

In his discussion of the faculty of aesthetic judgment, Immanuel Kant refers to beauty as a normative, commonsensical form of value.[3] Beauty is the result of a pleasure that stems from the shared desirability of an object; it is contingent upon its conformity with social codes and cultural norms. In this respect, the economy implied by beauty as an aesthetic category com-

---

2   *New Oxford American Dictionary*, version 2.2.1 (built 143.1)
3   Kant, Immanuel (1951 [1790]), *Critique of Judgment*, trans. J.H. Bernard, London and New York: Hafner Publications, section 22.

plies with the supply-and-demand principle that governs the traditional market environment. The beauty of something, that is, the degree of its refinement in complying with the commonly agreed, codified norms, reflects its economic value in comparison to other objects of the same kind. In Kant's framing, beauty is normative. As it enters the circulation of commodities, beauty itself and its value become measurable.

For example, think of the value of a design object. The design process must do more than resolve functional issues structured by social relationships. It must also reflect the social codes that are produced within these social relations. The value of the design object is, then, contingent upon its capacity to respond to these socially constructed functions and relations. Yet, the notion of beauty as such neither entirely explains aesthetic affections nor sufficiently unravels the production and circulation of aesthetic objects, because it does not untangle the production or transformation of norms.

Kant introduces the notion of the sublime in order to explain the entirely different set of affections we derive from a work of art. Sublime is different; it is what falls out of the threshold of common sense. Thus, it transcends aesthetic judgment shaped by common sense. According to Jean François Lyotard, sublime is something that has not yet been seen, is not yet known, and thus is not yet coded into social norms.[4] It is uncanny in the sense that it doesn't provide the comfortable pleasure beauty does. On the contrary, it violates the norms that beauty is grounded upon, and thrills us by not fulfilling our commonsense expectations, throwing us into unknown territory. Two constitutive aspects of the sublime are important to my discussion. The first is its newness and thus temporariness, that is, anything new, different, not yet known as such eventually becomes recognized and coded into existing social language upon its impact. The second is its immeasurability: as long as its newness makes its occurrence unique, the sublime is beyond comparison, making it also immeasurable.

Cool resembles sublime in this respect. I argue that cool functions as a substitute for sublime in the cultural field. It is an intervention into the banality of everyday culture by a new signifier, or a syntactical disruption

---

4 Lyotard, Jean-François (1984), *The Postmodern Condition: A Report on Knowledge*, trans. Geoff Bennington and Brian Massumi, Minneapolis: University of Minnesota Press.

of the signification process by a new arrangement of existing social codes. This is why cool is embraced by subcultural forms or subaltern identities—if not directly produced by them. As Dick Hebdige's famous analysis shows, subcultural style appears as a set of codes, a new formula for coolness that challenges the hegemonic signification regime by either shifting the relations between signifiers, or introducing new ones.[5]

When the work of art falls within the circulation of commodities in modern times, it subverts the notion of use value that governs market economy. It becomes an absolute commodity, a commodity that is beyond value, as it appears in terms of the "pricelessness of a great work of art." Antoon van den Braembussche points to Baudrillard and Baudelaire's political affirmation of absolute commodity. Being "beyond value," it carries the potential to subvert the market economy that it is forced to enter.[6] By embodying an "indifference towards utility and value, towards instrumental and intrinsic value, towards exchange and use value," absolute commodity imposes a crisis on the rationalities of economic value.[7] Yet, Braembussche warns about the pitfalls of Baudrillard's reaffirmation: the contestation embodied in the absolute commodity as such may not necessarily lead to the conquest of the sublime over the logic of value. Such absolute commodity can potentially be caught up in the logic of commodity fetishism, while pushing it to the extreme in order to transcend it. In Lyotard's words, "[i]n this way, one thinks that one is expressing the spirit of the times, whereas one is merely reflecting the spirit of the market. Sublimity is no longer in art, but in speculation on art."[8] We frequently witness the leap Lyotard warns about in elite art markets, where the speculative value is succeeded by an actual price that symbolizes the fact that some can even afford the priceless.

---

5   Hebdige, Dick (1988), *Subculture. The Meaning of Style. New Accents*. London and New York: Routledge.
6   Van den Braembussche, Antoon (1997), "The Value of Art," in *The Value of Culture: On the Relationship between Economics and Arts*, ed. Arjo Klamer, Amsterdam: Amsterdam University Press, pp. 31-43, p. 40.
7   Ibid. p. 41.
8   Lyotard, Jean-François (1989), "The Sublime and the Avant/Garde," in *The Lyotard Reader*, ed. Andrew Benjamin, Oxford and Cambridge: Blackwell, p. 210.

The parallelism between the meanings of the sublime in the realm of aesthetics and cool in the realm of everyday culture is followed by a similarity in the way the artifacts carrying their attributes circulate in the market environment, the economic value they translate into. Particularly, two intertwined constitutive characteristics of the sublime, its temporariness and its immeasurability, are crucially important when we consider cool as its substitute in popular cultural practices. Because by mimicking these characteristics, cool also creates an economy that resembles that of the sublime, and as soon as it starts to circulate in the market environment, the object of cool becomes an absolute commodity as such.

II. POST-FORDISM AND GLOBAL CULTURE INDUSTRY

One of the distinct features of the new form of capitalism is a new productive logic that transposes aesthetic values into economic production. Post-fordism, in this sense, not only refers to a global reconfiguration of production sites and markets, the shifting of industrial production to underdeveloped peripheries where there is an abundance of cheap labor, and the concentration of administrative functions in global finance centers, but also to a qualitative shift in productive labor processes and forms of value. In post-fordist capitalism, the hegemonic form of productive labor increasingly shifts from the model of unskilled labor deployed in the factory, to a new type that bears cognitive, linguistic and affective qualities.[9] Productive activities, as such, used to be confined to factories as the ultimate sites of economic production in the fordist model. In post-fordism, economic productivity spreads into every sphere of everyday life, and becomes inseparable from other social activities, including reproduction and leisure.[10] This in turn effectively shapes social relations, even primary or intimate ones. The economic value labor processes are entangled with, is also expressed in different terms. Unlike fordist operational logic, post-fordist

---

9   Lazzarato, Maurizio (1996), "Immaterial Labor," in *Radical thought in Italy: A Potential Politics*, ed. Paolo Virno and Michael Hardt, Minneapolis: University of Minnesota Press, pp. 132-146.
10 Deleuze, Gilles (1992), "Postscript on the Societies of Control," *October* 59, pp. 3-7.

industry is no longer directed towards producing merely simple commodities that bear use value. Instead, it produces more complex commodities: brands, events, life-styles, and things that appear to consumers as "social" and "aesthetic" experiences.[11]

In this respect, post-fordism reverses the condition that is critically identified by Theodor Adorno and Max Horkheimer as culture industry.[12] Culture industry, in Adorno and Horkheimer's criticism, refers to the mature state of modern capitalism, in which not only subsistence related social activities and economic production in general are defined by industrial mass production, but mass produced commodities also invade the cultural field, and define social reproduction. For Adorno and Horkheimer, the grave threat culture industry poses against enlightenment ideas is that commodities impose their sameness onto the social subjects who consume them, and thus reproduce conformist and docile social identities. In response, Scott Lash and Celia Lury interpret the transformation of the culture industry as a new form of cultural production and circulation, into a global culture industry where, according to them, brands replace mass produced cultural commodities, things replace representations and difference replaces identity.[13]

According to Lash and Lury, whether it is subsistence related or a cultural artifact, a commodity has a finitude that ultimately refers to use value. The exchange value of a commodity is an abstraction of its use value, which becomes expressed in another abstract equivalent, which is money. Therefore, exchange value is in fact a question of quantity that is derived from the quality of use value—which means that the value of commodities have an abstract equivalence, expressed in terms of money, which makes them measurable against each other in the same market environment. In its finitude, a commodity is "a single, discrete, fixed product" whereas, the brand is the "source of production," which "instantiates itself in a range of

---

11   Lash, Scott and Celia Lury (2007), *Global Culture Industry: The Mediation of Things*. Cambridge, UK, and Malden, MA: Polity, pp. 4-10.
12   Adorno, Theodor and Max Horkheimer, "Culture Industry: Enlightenment as Mass Deception," in *Dialectics of Enlightenment: Philosophical Fragments (1993 [1944])*, New York: Continuum, pp. 94-136.
13   Lash and Lury (2007), *Global Culture Industry*, p.6.

products," which is "generated across a range of products."[14] Unlike the commodity whose value is determined in reference to the use value generated by its consumption, the value of a brand is related to its productive potential. In the economy of brands, the reproduction of codes, meanings, differences and identities overlaps with the production of economic value. Commodities are "homogeneities," according to Lash and Lury, they "only have value in the way they resemble every other commodity," whereas brands "are not alike," they "have value only in their difference—their distinctiveness—from other brands."[15]

In this way, Lash and Lury's exposition of global culture industry contextualizes the profit motive in the transformation of economic logic. Unlike commodities, the value of brands is not limited; brands keep on producing an almost endless range/series of products which become things that imply difference in their circulation, and therefore embody a value that makes the discussion of their cost (and thus their price) irrelevant. They become part of lifestyles, meaning a life-long consumption pattern in terms of marketing. That is, when you sell a brand to a consumer, this potentially means that you have made a business deal with an indefinite future.

Lash and Lury's work also contextualizes the economic function of the cool in this new model. Cool, in the way I associated it with the notion of sublime above, is that difference that is essentially productive of value in the economy of brands. Difference is necessary for the brand, yet it implies an almost ideal form (that can only be approximated in reality) in the sense that, as soon as it is expressed and materialized in the thing—the industrial, mass produced commodity—it becomes the same, due to the nature of that very thing. Therefore, while difference as such is endlessly productive of economic value, it also has to be reproduced constantly, endlessly. The vagueness of cool facilitates this type of endless reproduction; anything can be cool because it potentially refers to something else. The cool of the previous decade can be cool again now to the degree it has been abandoned for being not-so-cool in the last decade. When coolness that is implied by smartness (in whatever form it materializes in) has been saturated enough, even simple stupidity can be cool—as shown by the clothing brand Diesel's

---

14   Ibid.
15   Ibid.

advertisement campaign since 2011.[16] Cool, in this sense, refers to the stripping off of the subalternity of the different, and its domestication under the economy of brands.

III. WAYS OF DOING

Whenever we discuss the economy of art and culture, the overwhelming anomaly of the value embodied in the material existence of the absolute commodity forces us to preoccupy ourselves with the sublime object. We are compelled to inquire upon the effects of such sublimity on the circulation of the object as it shatters laws of supply and demand, use value and exchange value. With an understandable fascination for such formidable intervention in the capitalist rationale, critical cultural studies, and social theory from Adorno and Horkheimer to Pierre Bourdieu have been concerned with the disjunction and resulting crisis of value between the work of art and the cultural commodity.[17]

Scholars of the Birmingham School of Cultural Studies, on the other hand, saw popular culture as a site of social reproduction where codes and meanings were produced, rather than centering their inquiry on the production and circulation of cultural commodities. By paying attention to the ideological processes and temporalities in the field of popular culture, Birmingham cultural studies made a unique contribution to thinking beyond and beneath the cultural economy, without the shadow of the cultural commodity. Following Stuart Hall, we have to consider the production of meaning (and therefore the production of all kinds of aesthetic forms) as labor process, and try to understand the political economy of culture not by focusing on the products (commodities or brands) but by looking into the production relations.[18] In other words, the question concerning the political

---

16 See "The Official Be Stupid Philosophy" advertisement video and Diesel ad campaign: http://www.diesel.com/be-stupid/ (accessed 15 April 2014).
17 Bourdieu, Pierre (1984), *Distinction: A Social Critique of the Judgement of Taste*, Cambridge, Mass.: Harvard University Press.
18 See Stuart Hall (1980), "Encoding/decoding," in *Culture, Media, Language*, ed. Stuart Hall, Dorothy Hobson, Andrew Love and Paul Willis, London: Hutchinson, pp. 128-38.

economy of culture is not only "what is produced?" but also "how is it produced?" because the relationship of economic production in this field is simultaneously the relationship of social reproduction.

In the modern era, contemporary art has been a site of resistance and contestation against capitalism, not only by harboring regimes of representation that challenge capitalist value systems, but also by providing alternative technologies of production and alternative labor processes. In this sense, the work of art is not merely an absolute commodity that escapes capitalist value even when it is commodified.[19] The more important challenge the work of art provides lies in the way that it harbors multiple logics of production, creative strategies, assemblages of ways of doing—all of which are resistant to, and surpass those of capitalism, by being productive of something that cannot be contained or ordered by the capitalist rationale. When we look into the social relations and creative labor practices deployed in aesthetic production throughout the long twentieth century, it becomes clear that such temporalities constituted alternative ontologies of labor. They made use of and produced gestures and activities, practices and procedures that are alternative to those of modern capitalist industrial production, and the market economy of the same period.

In other words, it was not only the exchange value of a Jackson Pollock painting (when it entered the art market as an object) that shattered the modern economic logic, but it was also the creative process, the gesture that Pollock's artistic practice embodied, its methodical randomness and absolute contingency. Pollock's work of art rose in this framework as an impenetrable alternative organization of productive knowledge, skills and activities challenging the dehumanizing Taylorist ontology of industrial production.

In a different temporal and geographical context, but in a similar way, Bauhaus appeared as a creative gesture that meticulously formulated the idea of design around the essential functions of an object, and also disciplined the creative activity itself in its most physical/bodily form. A striking

---

19 We need to keep in mind that a significant number of threads in various modern art movements were self-consciously invested in developing strategies against commodification of the works of art. Part of the artistic strategy in Fluxus's *happening* format, for instance, was not to create a product that could be commodified after the temporality of the aesthetic experience itself.

example of the latter is that Bauhaus members had to begin the day with physical exercises.[20] Such alternative technologies of production were perhaps best embodied in Godard's concept of "process" in its diametrical opposition to Pollock—in that, after spending a year in Africa with a video camera, he returned empty handed and said he couldn't find an image. Even idleness and boredom can be a valuable strategic resource for creative production during modern times, as punk has exemplified.

Each creative formula—its procedures, gestures, contingencies, tactics and strategies not only inscribe a different temporality of production, but also envelope it with a different ethos. For example, Sergei Eisenstein and Dziga Vertov, two filmmakers from the early years of the USSR, belonged to the same ideological camp, were both involved in the constructivist movement and used the same tools. Yet, each had a different idea of what cinema should be, each had a different way of making a film. In their artistic practice, both developed formulations constituting a different ethos that challenged the hegemonic ethos of Thomas Edison's emerging cinema industry at the time. Regardless of the fact that whether or not their products entered the market economy in the end, each creative logic brought along different sets of creative processes and procedures.

If we were to rethink creative labor processes as ways of doing, as technologies in an expanded sense, they would include cognitive, linguistic and affective processes, and extend towards other communicative instances and other forms of social exchange. Sites of production as such, have also been sites of social reproduction, as well as sites of resistance where social codes and subjectivities are shaped and reproduced in ways different from the hegemonic political rationale. The sphere of cultural and artistic production has been marked by other ways of doing throughout the modern era. The art market is concerned with absolute commodities, produced in ways that distinguish them from mass products, and the speculative value derived from the sublimity of the art work. The artist myth, for example—the artist as the creative/mad/genius—directly separates and affirms the artists' ways of doing from that of the rest of the real world.

Whereas, while resembling the sublime economy of the absolute commodity, and incorporating a value that is derived from the immeasurability

---

20 Scharenberg, Swantje (2003), "Physical education in the Bauhaus, 1919-33," *The International Journal of the History of Sport* 20 (3), pp. 115-127.

of difference in the field of cultural production, the economy of cool does not leave space for such other ways of doing and other ethos attached to them. The difference of the brand is produced in corporate offices within nine-to-five work days, through the proletarianization of creative labor—perhaps no longer in Taylorist assembly lines, but by similarly uniform and universally applicable creative asset management strategies. In other words, the work of art is necessarily produced in another economy before it enters the market, otherwise it wouldn't be possible to produce it as a mass commodity. Cool can be designed and produced as a mass commodity within industrial capitalist production cycles, as long as the same production cycles can encode the commodity in its public circulation. This is in fact not difficult at all within today's oligopolistic media markets in which a few major players also have close financial/administrative ties with other industries.

IV. EVERY MAN FOR HIMSELF AND GOD AGAINST ALL

The post-fordist subjugation of difference to capitalist economy as a source of value is intertwined with a transformation in liberalism as a logic of government. The public debates and left-wing criticism of neoliberalism often points to the privatization of public resources, deregulation of markets under pro-business incentives, and anti-welfare economic policies. Whereas, as Michel Foucault points out, just as traditional liberalism once appeared as a social design based on the market model, neoliberalism also emerges as an overarching social program rather than as a set of ruthlessly anti-social economic policies.[21] Aimed at transforming the social fabric,

---

21 Foucault, Michel (2007), *Security, Territory, Population: Lectures at the Collège de France*, New York: Picador, pp. 101-128. Also see Lemke, Thomas Lemke (2001), "The Birth of Bio-Politics'—Michel Foucault's Lecture at the Collège de France on Neo-Liberal Governmentality," *Economy & Society* 30 (2), pp. 190-207; Gordon, Colin (1991), "Governmental Rationality: An Introduction," in *The Foucault Effect. Studies in Governmentality: with two lectures by and an interview with Michel Foucault*, ed. Graham. Burchell,

expressed in a new set of priorities in cultural policies over the past three decades, this new logic of government coupled with post-fordist economic formulas to eliminate ways of doing and ethos other than those imposed by the markets.

Michel Foucault associates the rise of liberal governmentality with an economist logic starting to dominate the political sphere. This new type of political power appears as almost pedagogical. It relies on the model of managing a household, a multilayered care-taking activity that orients towards acceptable ways of managing the individuals, goods and wealth in the family. In this regard, this pedagogy, what he calls the art of government, takes on an economic logic. The essential issue for the establishment of the art of government, Foucault notes, is the introduction of economy into political practice. Eighteenth century liberalism is founded on this premise. What was suggested as the logic of the art of government becomes a social rationale in eighteenth century liberalism. As already prescribed in sixteenth century political thought, the same logic of the right disposition of things applies to each and every social subject to govern himself, his family, his business and his relations with others, in the absence of an absolute, external, singular and transcendent governor. What becomes a social rationale seeks to provide a continuity at all layers of social life, from administrative and public affairs to taking care of one's own body and managing one's self.[22]

Eighteenth century liberalism formulates a notion of the market according to this rationale, replacing the common good that was once the locus of social life in sovereign power regimes. The market is found as the absolute expression of this rationale in classical liberalism. It is formulated as the social space of free exchange between rational individuals who automatically, naturally and conveniently make decisions. The invisible hands of the market, and the supply and demand mechanism, determine what is convenient for all in the absence of an outside intervention. The market is an open system that can contain all the social interactions, all the social exchanges. It is based on differentials among the participants, makes the exchange

---

Colin Gordon and Peter Miller, Chicago: University of Chicago Press, pp. 41-42.

22 Foucault, Michel (1991), "Governmentality," in *The Foucault Effect*, pp. 87-104.

possible, and such exchange also brings the successful negotiation of differences. It takes care of everyone, as long as each participant takes care of her/his own. In this regard, if the political problem is conveniently defined as the right disposition of things, then, the market provides a highly operational model for politics—in fact, a model that is functional to the degree that it can effectively substitute for politics. If the decision-making processes concerning social and public affairs (as well as the manners and forms that individuals participate in, in these social and public affairs) are determined by the market for the convenience of all. This means that previously formulated functions of administrative apparatuses have to be reconfigured accordingly. To this end, according to classical liberalism, the public is formulated as nothing but a negotiation of private interests, and the state becomes the limit, the outside of the market, whose only function is to protect the market without intervening in its "natural" dynamics and "natural" development.

Although it was surrounded by market and other social institutions, arts and culture as a site of social production (along, perhaps with the sphere of academia, knowledge production, and the sphere of intimate relations, social reproduction) was kept out of this new political logic, and at least to a certain degree, was left to be governed by its own productive devices in modern times. According to Foucault, in Adam Smith's formulation, the market was not merely an economic but a social model.[23] Smith concluded that there were moments of social life that served the public good in ways that could not be evaluated through the market's invisible hands. The labor processes that belonged to philosophy, arts, culture, and perhaps to a degree, even scientific works, were defined by their own (often plural) productive logics which referred to little or no immediate utilitarian value, and the value of the products of these labor processes remained immeasurable by the market. In European countries, artistic and cultural production was defined as a privileged field in social life and supported by public funds, which guaranteed its semi-autonomy from the market. This was partly an effect of the enlightenment project, partly an effect of more pragmatic welfare policies. In the example of Austria, this includes the involvement of monarchies and aristocracies. In the US, such public funding is indirectly

---

23   Foucault, Michel (2010), *The Birth of Biopolitics: Lectures at the Collège de France*, New York: Picador.

established through the legal/economic concept of non-profit organization. Particularly after World War II, arts and culture funds in the US have been effectively sustained by the funding mechanisms of tax-exempt private foundations, in order to balance the cultural effects of a profit-oriented mass media.

However, the semi/relative autonomy that arts and culture enjoy within liberal governmental rationale has been suspended in a new formulation that has become the hegemonic logic of government over the past few decades. Foucault's analysis points to a break in liberal governmentality after World War II, as a misguided reaction to modern forms of authoritarianisms.[24] According to the Frankfurt School's Marxian analysis, the rise of fascism was a product of capitalism under specific circumstances, i.e. the lack of access to an outside to expand to, both as a market and in terms of colonial resources. Therefore, for the Frankfurt School, the resulting authoritarian turn was a failure of the free market economy and liberalism.[25] Ordoliberals, and in particular the Freiburg School, on the other hand, believed that fascism was not a product of the free market and liberal economy, but inversely, it was the result of their absence. For them, the dissolution of democracy under the Nazis was the inevitable outcome of certain policies and social formations that prevented the establishment of liberalism and a true market economy.

The Ordoliberal interpretation of the rise of authoritarianism as a consequence of the prevention of the development of free market and liberal economic conditions led them to reconsider the key formulation of classical liberalism. According to eighteenth century liberalism, the market had a quasi-natural quality. It was seen as a natural outcome of the social interactions which it tended to envelope. Thus the market was expected to develop and sustain itself naturally on its own dynamics, unless there was external intervention, such as that from the state. In this formulation, the role of the state, as I have already mentioned, was to protect the market's freedom without intervening.

Unlike the Frankfurt School, whose fundamental alternative was between capitalism and socialism, the Freiburg School's crucial distinction was between liberalism and various sorts of state interventionism. Accord-

---

24   Lemke (2001), "The Birth of Bio-Politics'."
25   Ibid.

ing to the Ordoliberals, not only fascism but also socialism and Keynesianism represented varying degrees of authoritarianism and threatened liberty.[26] In the view of the Ordoliberals, these authoritarian political forms stemmed from social forces rooted in collective social experience, they hijacked state power to annihilate market conditions and social liberties. The Ordoliberals thought that if social forces had the capacity to prevent the market from developing freely and engendering these authoritarian interventions, then the founding thesis of classical liberalism, i.e. that the market is a natural extension/ground for the social, would need to be revised.

Thus, the Freiburg School refashioned liberalism by replacing the Dionysian soul of eighteenth century narrative with an Apollonian character. According to the Ordoliberal revision, the market was not a quasi-natural social phenomenon but an ideal form. As such, it couldn't be left to grow on its own, but had to be actively cultivated, constituted and maintained by political interventions. Moreover, according to their interpretation, as shown by the fascism and socialism examples, social relations were anti-competitive by their very nature, and the inherent social tendency for collectivism would eventually bring various forms of authoritarianism. Ordoliberalism suggested that fascism and socialism were eventual consequences of intrinsic collectivist tendencies in the social field. This interpretation led the Ordoliberals to reformulate the function of state in regard to the market and public life. The political interventions that the actual market needed in order to better approximate its ideal form, could only be organized by the state. In other words, according to the Ordoliberals, the state had to intervene in the social in order to prevent it from intervening in the market.

Foucault also draws attention to an important shift in the key term around which the conception of the market becomes organized. For classical liberalisms of the eighteenth and nineteenth century, market meant exchange. *Laissez faire* was the condition of free exchange among individuals, and the state had to protect this free exchange from the outside. The neoliberal conception, while breaking away with the naturalism of eight-

---

26 Foucault, Michel (2010), *The Birth of Biopolitics*, pp. 116-121.

eenth and nineteenth century liberalisms, also reorganized the meaning of the market around the notion of competition.[27]

This conceptual shift brought important consequences. Once the market's engine was defined as competition, various forms of equilibrium became problematic in neoliberal discourse because they simply minimized the incentives for competition. Examples were market equilibrium in the purely economic sense, where exchange took place harmoniously via supply and demand mechanisms; or social equality, which imposed a fair and egalitarian distribution of resources among social subjects. Economic and social differentials were keys to competition. Market was thought of as a gross plane of inequality on which the differentials among individual actors made them compete against each other, in order to achieve relatively better positions against each other in their inequality. Perhaps the best phrase that summarizes the neoliberal vision is Werner Herzog's film title *Every Man For Himself and God Against All* (1974), based on the story of Kaspar Hauser, a savage young boy who suddenly appears on the market square of a town and has to learn how to speak and how to survive in civil life. Everybody is equal before a great inequality, everybody competes with each other to survive it.

While post-fordist economic incentives have been reorganizing global capitalism at the structural level, neoliberal policies have been reshaping the government institutions around the globe. Cultural production in the west has been transformed over the past three decades under the post-fordist market conditions on the one hand, and under neoliberal cultural policies on the other. Neoliberal cultural policies have not only decreased public funding of the arts and culture, they have also allocated the available funds to initialize and develop market structures in the cultural arena, rather than guaranteeing its freedom from the market. Under the buzzword creative industries, the privileged status of cultural and artistic production has been redefined in a joint discourse by neoliberal and post-fordist initiatives. It shifted from being indexed to public good towards economic productivity. As such, spaces of cultural production and creative labor processes become sterilized from their differences and incorporated into the economic cycles of the global culture industry. This model allows for differences only if they speak a common language. Every creative person has to have a

---

27   Ibid.

portfolio, one or two concepts, a well-defined research agenda (or works-in-progress), a neat haircut and a briefcase, and lots of contacts in the industry. Whether you are an artist, a writer, a scholar, or an actual soccer player, you have to "bend it like Beckham;" every smile should be a toothpaste advertisement.

V. FROM THINGS TO EVENTS AND BACK

Yet, how could the cool, the difference in other words, with all its immeasurability, fit into such an economy without dragging it into a crisis, become part of such banality without contesting it? In order to make sense of this subsumption, we have to first examine the political economy of the global culture industry, and look into how it has been structurally transformed over the past few decades in terms of operational scales, industrial practices and business strategies.

Today a very large share of the US media market is occupied by four-five global corporations, whose holdings span across a variety of media markets vertically and horizontally through subsidiaries that have considerable market share in other cultural/linguistic territories, and whose economic interests are directly or indirectly related with other sectors.[28] The incorporation of cool into the economic flows of the global culture industry is made possible by an operational scale of media industries that can mobilize

---

28 As Robert McChesney recognizes, it proves somehow useless to seek for and provide precise statistical data when it comes to assessing corporate holdings and structures in media industries. The mergers, buyouts, horizontal associations and shifts in sub-sectors etc. happen so rapidly that, even the data collected a few months ago loses its precision. The fact remains the same, though. Since the mid 2000's, over 80% of the US media market has been dominated by a handful of corporations in various compositions. See Waterman McChesney, Robert (1999), "Rich Media Poor Democracy: Communication Politics in Dubious Times," in *The History of Communication*, Urbana: University of Illinois Press; Lutz, Ashley (2012), "These 6 corporations control 90% of the media in America," *Business Insider*, 14 June 2012; Freepress, "Who owns the media?": http://www.freepress.net/ownership/chart (accessed 15 April 2014).

integrated marketing campaigns and cross-promotion strategies at an unprecedented level of intensity and sophistication. The story of the movie *Titanic* is an example of how a sunken movie project can not only be retrieved, but made cool and hugely profitable with an aggressive cross-promotion campaign.[29] Today, the promotion of a blockbuster film starts before its production, and by the time the movie hits the theaters, it has already become a social event. The new economic logic of global culture industry that Lash and Lury dissect actually runs on two conditions that were not available in the culture industry Adorno and Horkheimer criticized earlier. The first is the level of penetration new media technologies assert over everyday, primary social relations. The second is the concentration of capital and oligopolistic economic structures that assert a practical control over a media market overlapping with everyday life.

Under these circumstances, the global media industry can create events that can substitute the effect of the sublime and the cool through an artificially constructed novelty around ordinary and banal things. On the one hand, the global culture industry infuses the circulation of material commodities with aesthetic experiences. What Kant called beauty has become an essential form of value in ordinary commodities, and thus has turned objects of utility into design or life-style objects. Lash and Lury point to this transformation as things replacing representations.[30] On the other hand, the sublime, the aesthetic affect of the work of art, has been detached from its object and constructed outside of it. If need be, it has even been constructed in its absence, and often as an event. Carrying the effect of the sublime, without the intervention of the work of art, an event can now be incorporated into lifestyles, brands, and social experiences. In other words, an exhibition, a biennial, a performance, a show can essentially and seamlessly become integral to capitalist accumulation regimes. What we have, then, is a passage from the enchanting novelty of the absolute commodity to the absolute novelty of an enchanted event.

The enchanting novelty of the event substitutes the experience of the sublime by being akin to it. It constructs the newness of the present: "it is

---

29   See Welkos, Robert W., "The $200 Million Lesson of Titanic," *Los Angeles Times*, 11 February 1998; Garrett, Diane, "Big-budget bang-ups," *Variety* , 20 April 2007.

30   Lash and Lury (2007), *Global Culture Industry*, pp. 4-10.

what is happening now, what has not been, and what will not be."[31] Newness as such shatters the logic of value as does the sublime. The pure novelty of the event, its temporality, makes it beyond measure and therefore beyond value. Being there, a part of that event, living it is a priceless experience. The post-modern spectacle distributes such value that is beyond measure into a chain of associated commodities and services that altogether construct the event: the merchandise, the tickets, the guided tour, the memorabilia, etc. The products that enable you to experience the event, and turn that experience into memories, in contrast with the pricelessness of the event, come with a price tag.

The importance of the sublime lies in its generative power, as Lyotard recognizes. The unrepresentable presented by the sublime, the uncanny difference it introduces, expands the limits of language, our sphere of representations and cognitive capacities, while its temporality quickly fades away. The event that presents itself as an experience akin to the sublime has a similar effect in post-fordist cycles of economy: it not only directly refers to a chain of associated commodities and services, but also expands in time in both directions. It becomes an effect that turns locations and spaces into places and sites, seeds future experiences, and begins to mobilize future commodities and services. In turn, it formulates and facilitates life-styles, brands and eternal consumption patterns.

VI. THE NEW BYZANTIUM

Events as such also serve to incorporate into the global flows of capital locations that were once culturally and financially peripheral, i.e. Istanbul, Dubai, Rio de Janeiro, etc. As has happened in Istanbul, large-scale spectacles such as the Formula 1 races, the biennials, various international art and culture festivals, and gallery districts that continuously present novelties, reintegrate the once peripheral city into the contemporary world market. These events and scenes refashion the privileged districts of these urban sites into something found in any other contemporary city, often by offering

---

31 Harutyunyan, Angela, Ozgun, Aras and Eric Goodfield (2011), "Event and Counter-Event: The Political Economy of the Istanbul Biennial and Its Excesses," *Rethinking Marxism*, 23 (4), pp. 478-495.

a patchwork of scenographies: business districts that resemble Downtown Manhattan without a shabby smelly Chinatown; gallery districts that look Parisian; music venues with the air of London. Or as in Williamsburg in New York City, in the absence of a displaced midscale industry, prewar warehouses were built from scratch to offer a luxurious loft living experience to local affluent young professionals. These event-scenes plaster over the inherent inequalities of the social fabric with coolness and make these sites cool on a global scale.

Yet, contemporariness becomes more than a refashioning theme for urban space, it also functions as a political discourse to compensate for, or counteract the failed modernization processes of the past. Modernization has been a hegemonic vision for third world politics, regardless of whether the site embodied a socialist or capitalist industrialization. Industrialization, as a key component of modernization, does not refer strictly to a form of economic production, i.e. factories, but also to the series of social, urban, legal and ideological dispositions that come with it. In the case of Turkey, Turgut Özal, Prime Minister of Turkey from 1983 to 1989, was to bypass this issue, and reformulate the idea of modernity around a set of social consumption patterns rather than socio-economic production processes. This was, of course, only possible under the circumstances of the specific political discontinuity imposed by the 1981 military coup. Beginning with Özal's post-military government, almost all parties and governments in Turkish politics have indexed their success to the achievement of contemporariness defined in vague terms: from bidding on the Olympic Games, World Fairs, and various international sports events to hosting cultural events, such as the Istanbul Biennial, Istanbul's international cinema festival and jazz festival, and most recently, its selection as the European Capital of Culture in 2010.

During the last decade in Turkey, even the conservative AKP government who rigidly controlled or heavy-handedly censored even the smallest criticism of everyday culture, appeared to have tolerance and even compassion when it came to international contemporary art events. In contrast, the misery of the shanty towns still surrounding the city, the poverty of the precariat that fueled the new post-fordist economy, the gross violations of the very basic human rights of the underprivileged masses, the flames of an acute civil war burning in the distance in south-east Turkey could be ignored as *passé*, so long as the events that located Istanbul in the map of the contemporary world happened to be there, so long as the event-scenes infused the temporality of urban life with an undeniable sense of contemporariness for the urbanites. In Erdoğan's hands, Özal's rhetorical invention has become a whip that keeps drawing blood. Any criticism, whether from the left or right, is considered by the government a conspiracy against the imagination of contemporary Turkey, and as such merits death by gassing. The way that the Gezi resistance was handled by the Erdoğan government, is a case in point.

In other words, a self-referential notion of contemporariness not only mobilizes new economic resources and directly generates considerable financial flows, but it also incorporates an ideological intervention that works to bypass political criticism that points to new economic inequalities brought about by the post-fordist transformation. For a city and its people who have been desperately struggling to become modern for a few centuries now, being contemporary once again offers a value that is beyond the measure of political and economic reason.

The inequalities and political complications created by post-fordist economies in places like formerly peripheral sites like Turkey, particularly affect the precariat. This is the new precarious working class that provides the labor force for the local branches of the global culture industry in these cities. In Istanbul, after the new economy became consolidated, we witnessed a few outbursts of anger from this new working class as soon as they came to the bitter realization of their new socio-economic reality. It was the result of the failure of the socio-economic benefits promised to creative workers, artists, as well as to a new generation of well-educated technocrats, in return for the "gross national cool" they had been producing.[32] The intense protests against the eleventh edition of the Istanbul Biennial in 2011 constituted a significant moment in this context. The protesters saw the eleventh biennial as a socialist spectacle for the enjoyment of the rich and the tourists financed by the wealthy industrialist Koç Holding. They called for sabotage and vandalism. They criticized the working conditions of the precarious workers, such as those volunteering or working low-pay cultural service jobs in the biennial, showing the scale of the discontent felt by the

---

32 Nothing expresses cool as a privileged form of economic value in post-fordism as the witty title of Douglas McGray's uncritical article published in the May 2002 issue of *Foreign Policy* ("Japan's Gross National *Cool*.").

precariat towards the otherwise rosy development of the arts scene in the city.
During and after the protests, the public debates involving artists and intellectuals reflected a division within the creative community. To some, being against a high calibre art event was unjustifiable from a left-wing political perspective. As such, the critics must have been nationalist/conservatives who couldn't stomach the contemporary arts. This division itself reveals a condition we have already observed in western centers of cultural production: functioning as a part of the global culture industry, the creative sector develops its own internal conflicts and class dynamics. The tension and conflict of interests intrinsic to capitalism arise between managerial cadres of art institutions, and those who sell their creative labor under precarious work conditions. This division structures the field of artistic and cultural production.

VII. ETHOS

More recently, after no longer being able to pay the rent in the city's cool neighborhoods, to the gentrification of which they had been actively contributing over the past few decades, the precariat mobilized against an urban development project in Gezi Parkı. What started as a small scale, ordinary protest against the privatization of the urban commons quickly escalated into a massive rebellion that spread throughout most major cities and towns in Turkey. The escalation of the protests in the face of massive police brutality, the significance of this escalation and its brutal repression, and its eventual signaling of the end of AKP's ideological hegemony merits a lengthy discussion, which is unfortunately beyond the scope of the current chapter. However, I would like to emphasize one very important point: the Gezi Parkı protests brought an important novelty to Turkish radical politics. This may be very much related to the rapid popularization of the protests as well as to the unprecedented levels of brutality they received. Rather than making their voices heard and going home, the protesters reclaimed the urban commons that had been taken from them. They occupied the park and used it as a space to develop non-capitalist social relations and economic exchange, and to invent new and different ways of doing. The protest quickly turned into resistance. The tent camp not only successfully began to experiment with alternative technologies for creating, doing, and living that neoliberal politics had intended to eradicate forever, but the participants also enveloped these in an ethos that defied the political logic of representative democracy.

It was a powerful expression of a collective desire for another possible world, the spawns of alternative social practices such desire gave birth to, and the ethos of resistance that draw the wrath of AKP's neoliberalism upon itself in Gezi Parkı. This showed clearly that what constitutes an existential threat to brand economy is not the cheap knock-off's, imitations, or the surplus production that undercuts the value of the logo. Instead, it is social practices such as the Do-it-Yourself culture, non-capitalist mutual exchange, workers cooperatives, other forms production, circulation and other acts of communing that elude the regime of continuous consumption.

Post-fordism is not a monolithic economic prescription. It is an amalgamation of diverse strategies and tactics that emerged to overcome, incorporate or circumvent various sites of resistance that impose obstacles and crises upon modern capitalism.[33] The transformation of arts and culture into a privileged economic sector, as I tried to explain before, not only incorporates it into capitalist production, but further imposes a challenge to developing resistance strategies. Even the expression of subversive political and moral statements, which can no longer take place in any other corner of the public sphere, are welcomed in the very established and mainstream institutions of art and culture today because of their potential for eventfulness. In countries that have severe problems keeping up with the internationally recognized criteria of liberal political and economic rights, such as Turkey, human rights abuses are perceived almost as ordinary everyday affairs. Yet, banning an exhibition or show is perceived as an outrageous and unacceptable violation of freedom of expression. Artists living in "the free world" are now mostly free from direct and visible forms of censorship, and disciplinary and oppressive instruments of social control. In fact, the institutions and the media environment they work in encourage them to be even more transgressive, critical, edgy, and excessive. That is, as long as their creative production remains within the system of gallery displays, and

---

33 Hardt, Michael and Antonio Negri (2000), *Empire*, Cambridge, Mass.: Harvard University Press.

becomes incorporated into the production/consumption cycles of the global culture industry.[34]

And so, at that very moment when we find ourselves privileged social subjects, as artists and cultural producers, as almost "classless and free" subjects on the one hand, and the precariat of the world on the other, what question do we ask ourselves? We have few prospects outside the electronic sweatshops and gallery walls where we create events and contribute to that narrative, and where we also are exploited. How can we be cool without producing/contributing to the branding of the cool?

The Gezi Parkı protests and various similar acts of resistance across the globe give us a reference point in this regard. The beauty of that iconic *kırmızılı kadın* (woman in red) standing alone in front of the police line as her hair blew with the tear gas spray, the virtuosity of Çarşı fans in selling the armored vehicle they stole from the police online, the graffiti and slogans witty enough to give the most creative advertisement gurus a run for their money, were only a few of the many inspiring cool moments in the course of the Gezi Parki resistance. It was an ethos of resistance that marked the temporality of these events, and produced a cool, or multiple cools that cannot be repeated, decontextualized or appropriated by the postfordist economy. Erdoğan knows this best: after all the protesters are beaten, gassed and arrested, still haunted by the image of *kırmızılı kadın*, the Turkish riot police continues to wait in the now empty square.

Perhaps, we should start again by giving words their true meanings. In this case, by rethinking what we understand by the term cool. It is not a coincidence that cool was a significant term in the Black American culture of the early twentieth century. Despite the fact that the meaning of *cool* reflected the painful history and struggles of African Americans, it still signified a positive attribute. Yet it didn't refer to what was merely fashionable. It referred to a particular attitude, a calm audaciousness, cold indifference, calm infused with apathy.[35] In the history of Black American Culture, when the price of open rebellion was too high, keeping emotions under control, calmly refuting the power by being indifferent to it, being uncon-

---

34 Harutyunyan, Angela, Ozgun, Aras and Eric Goodfield (2011), "Event and Counter-Event."

35 Thompson, Robert Farris (1973), "An Aesthetic of the Cool," *African Arts* 7 (1), pp. 40-43; 64-67; 89-91.

cerned with it, became valuable. Therefore, in this context, although the cool attitude did not immediately refer to a style, it did come to mean a set of behaviors brought together within the ethos of resistance and survival. This eventually became embodied in the jazz music of the 1920s in the United States, as well as in other stylistic forms of Black Culture. In this sense, cool in its origins did not mean fashionable, as it does today. It was in the temporality of Black Culture, and then in that of the white countercultures it inspired (such as the Beatniks or Mods), that being cool acquired its mainstream meanings and became fashionable.

When we return cool to an ethical framework, and redefine the culture of cool around it, what remains before us is no longer a cool city, but instead a burgeoning concentration of global culture industry, no more a cool artist but a precarious worker. Cool, then, will be waiting to be done—not in the shopping malls and art galleries, but behind the barricades, in that occupied park in the middle of the city.

Reflections on the Panel "Working Poor or Working Deprived in Cool Istanbul?"

An Attempt at Collective Thought

ASLI ODMAN with Ayşe Berna Uçarol, Burcu Barakacı, Duygu Semiz, Fikriye Akgül, Melis Tantan, Mustafa Adnan Akyol and Zeycan Elarslan

What do a culture manager, an NGO employee, a marble mason, a *dershane*[1] teacher, an ex-insurance agent, a call center worker, an apparel worker, and an ex-employee of a foundation university[2] have to say to each other and to you? Can they make relevant statements about your and each another's work realities? How do the accounts of our work lives relate to the

1   *Dershane* has become one of the key institutions in the Turkish education system during the past 20-25 years. It is a private institution that supports public education by preparing students for various types of state-run central entrance exams, such as the multiple-choice exam for entrance into state universities, private foreign schools, high schools, and public servant entrance tests. This institution reflects the de-facto privatization trend of the public education system, and the ongoing precarization of education personnel.

2   Article 130 of the Turkish Constitution outlaws for-profit institutions in the higher education system. An institutional solution to this legal ban has been the 'foundation' university which is established by a foundation board consisting of private persons, in contrast to public universities founded by the state. Since the establishment of the first foundation university in 1984 their number has risen to 72, currently comprising more than forty percent of all universities in Turkey as of March 2014.

Photograph: Derya Özkan

"flamboyant" and "artsy-craftsy" representation of Istanbul, to borrow notions coined by the participants of this panel? In other words, is there something common among workplaces throughout the city, including plazas, call centers, universities, construction sites, offices, factories and *dershanes*, as seen from the perspective of the employees to which these places owe their existence? Considering that these workplaces are usually quite dissociated from one another, that they are usually not physically in touch, that they do not directly connect, although they do indirectly *serve each other*[3] by producing commodities, how can they relate to each other? In the panel we held on 8 November 2013 as part of the conference "Cool Istanbul: Urban Enclosures and Resistances," our goal, as the participants of the panel focusing on "Laboring Istanbul," was to investigate the commonalities and differences amongst workplaces situated side by side in the urban space, and to single out some discussion lines beyond the vision of city planners who draw, color and assign functions to map sections as industrial, commercial, touristic areas or business centers. The following is based on narratives by Ayşe Berna Uçarol, Burcu Barakacı, Duygu Semiz, Fikriye Akgül, Melis Tantan, Mustafa Adnan Akyol, Zeycan Elarslan and Aslı Odman, all residents and workers of Istanbul, telling us about the impact of the regimes of labor in the city, on their lives as worker subjects.

The aim of this panel was to create a platform for workers employed in both new and enduring economic sectors in Istanbul to share and compare their work experiences beyond the commonplace images associated with their sectors. The inspiration for my approach comes from *London Labour, London Poor*, a project by Henry Mayhew[4], an ambitious journalist meticulously documenting work experiences across various occupations actually present in a mature capitalist city at the end of the nineteenth century. I aspire to superpose the narratives told by the eight contributors to reunite the scattered labor realities of a fragmented city, without referring to concrete quotations by the panel participants. Instead, I will try to synthesize

---

3   As Bob Dylan says in his song "*Gotta Serve Somebody*." The song goes on "[...]But you're gonna have to serve somebody, yes indeed /You're gonna have to serve somebody/It may be the devil or it may be the Lord /But you're gonna have to serve somebody [...]".

4   Mayhew, Henry (1985 [1840]), *London Labor and the London Poor*, Selections made and introduced by Victor Neuburg, London: Penguin Classics.

their accounts in order to tentatively seek a common terminology. The ultimate aim of this summary is to modestly document a panel that was meant to serve as a platform to compare the working conditions and subjectivities of white and blue collar workers, so as to explore the thesis that global cities are witnessing processes of globalization, precarization, labor intensification and disqualification of the labor force.[5] That said, I also intend to touch upon possible commonalities among laborers, perceived and understood from the workers' perspective living in the city, which I handle from the perspective of the psychodynamics of working life, also called the approach of *souffrance au travail* (work misery) in the francophone tradition, a field of study so far not institutionalized in Turkey.[6] Finally, this panel aims to inquire whether there is an "alternative coolness" from below, a concept possibly emerging within collective structures organizing themselves at odds with the humanly inflicted inequality and misery on the shop floor, despite and likely thanks to, seemingly insurmountable difficulties.

The two sessions we held in November 2013 primarily led me to change the main title from "Working Cool, Working Poor" to "Working Poor or Working Deprived in Cool Istanbul?" The former title refers to the

---

5   For a condensed summary on labor in the global city see Sassen, Saskia (2005), "The Global City: Introducing a Concept," *Brown Journal of World Affairs* 11 (2), pp. 27-43.

6   Three of the founders and most prominent representatives of this field, who have combined the classical labor anthropology with the study of occupational diseases of all types (physical and psychological) are the health sociologist Annie Thébaud-Mony, the psychiatrist/psychoanalyst Christophe Déjours and the sociologist Vincent de Gauljac. Thébaud-Mony's book *Working May Severely Harm Your Health* (Travailler peux nuir gravement a votre santé) and de Gaulejac's *The Ill Managerial Society* (La societé malade de la géstion) was translated into Turkish in the past two years. See: Thébaud-Mony, Annie (2012), *Çalışmak Sağlığa Zararlıdır*, Istanbul: Ayrıntı; de Gaulejac, Vincent (2013), *İşletme Hastalığına Tutulmuş Toplum*, Istanbul: Ayrıntı. Christoph Dejours's 1998 book *Souffrance en France. La banalisation de l'injustice social* (Paris: éditions du Seuil) has been refered to several times as the "founding book" of the psychodynamics of work, yet awaits its translator and publishing house.

not necessarily spatially grounded literature about the "working poor,"[7] whereas the latter more effectively underscores the spatially shared but divided experiences running through the narratives. This exchange of experiences took place in a largely "unprocessed and direct" manner as we had held only one preparatory meeting beforehand. The panel demonstrated that there is a work anxiety that the images of cool Istanbul cover up, reverse and leave out. The presenters described this feeling with the notion "falling short of everything" or "deprivation." According to the narratives, working in cool Istanbul puts one in a deprived condition, both materially and spiritually. We have concluded by arguing that working in cool Istanbul creates some shared disadvantages for all workers, and the most commonly shared disadvantage is the feeling of being exposed to an insecure future regardless of the sector one might work in.

What actually compelled me to suggest this subject as a discussion topic was an aversion to a strict theoretical definition of the working class. Here, I do not depend on an old definition of the working class by investigating which workers live and work in which parts of Istanbul. According to this definition, urban space is a passive container housing workers. I do not approach space in such an essentialist manner.[8] My initial framework focused on working conditions, workplaces, perceptions and work miseries. I agree neither with neoclassical economics, which classifies the "worker" as a production factor in the three main sectors of agriculture, industry and services, nor with the deductive methods of a positivist Marxist approach, which sees the worker confined to the factory as *the* space of the worker par excellence, and glorifying manual laborers as the carriers of an ultimate work ethics. I perceive work both as a process weaving the workspace day

---

7   The United States Department of Labor, Bureau of Labor Statistics annually prepares profile reports on the "working poor." It indicates the official acceptance of this term as part of the formal economy. For a genealogical analysis of the concept for sample cases in the European context, see: Andress, Hans Jürgen and Henning Lohmann (2008), *The Working Poor in Europe: Employment, Poverty, and Globalization*, Cheltenham: Edward Elgar.

8   Radical geographers have contributed immensely to Marxist theory by exploring the concept of social space beginning with the 1960s. For an introduction to different contributions, see Soja, Edward (1989), *Postmodern Geographies: The Reassertion of Space in Critical Social Theory*, London: Verso Press.

in, day out with its routines ("ant legs"), and as the sum of a human being's concrete practices of all types, productive and reproductive, through which her/his space, body, habits, expectations and dreams are produced.

In the panel, we avoided analyses of "class" and "worker" that resemble post-mortem examinations, since they assume (through time and space) a non-changing essence for the working class, and impose this definition on the changing realities of the production relations, and thus reify them.[9] We also tried to avoid a theoretical reproduction of social divisions as "differences and identities," as they come into being in our urban lives in between spaces of production. After all, the city is the sum of networks made up of the relations between factories, construction sites, free production zones, plazas, hospitals, *dershanes*, universities, workshops, households, shipyards, call centers, schools, and streets. Istanbul is our framework, our relational space. We live and produce the city; it is the ground we share. It is that which makes our paths cross and diverge from each other. During the panel, we attempted to investigate the connections as well as the lack of connections between singular workspaces scattered throughout the city. We inquired into the relations between workplace realities and the dominant images of Istanbul produced as part of the city branding at a larger scale.

To understand the material production of Istanbul, we focused on eight of the production areas and workplaces the participants brought to the table. The commodities produced in these spaces are highly diverse: Buildings, education, insurance, shirts, works of art, social projects, and communication. The city produces unity in an indirect manner by providing us with the means to produce these commodities, some of which are exported and consumed by the global market, although most are consumed in the local market by other workers. Nonetheless, spatial and symbolic arrangements make it more difficult to bring the producers and consumers together in practice and discourse. The metropolis also corresponds to the superimpositions, distances and barriers that prevent us from seeing associations and alliances.

---

9   For an encompassing discussion, see Wright, Eric Olin (Ed.) (2005): *Approaches to Class Analysis*. Cambridge University Press. For a condensed summary of the Turkish scholarly debates, see Öğütle,Vefa Saygın (2010), "Pozitivist-Marksist Sınıf Kavrayışı ve Sınıf Deneyimlerindeki Açmazları," *Praksis* 24, pp. 77-93.

The workers, the owners of the labor force, comprise the largest part of Istanbul's population, offering/selling their labor and getting paid either in per diem allowances, project-based payments or monthly wages. Obviously, our goal is not to pretend that the great socio-spatial distance between some of these workers is non-existent. We do not purport to hide behind the shortcut "we are all workers, we are all laborers," ignoring or underestimating different experiences and stories. We are aware that cities formed within capitalism survive by continuously dividing and restructuring all labor processes and the economic whole, and by generating surplus value in these processes. Differentiation is constitutive of the city, and is an essential part of its human-made nature. The spatial projection of this differentiation usually implies serious social segregation issues and great physical distances. Sometimes social gulfs may also appear between spatially close realities.

The range of spaces mentioned throughout the sessions varies from a luxurious housing estate construction site in Halkalı, to the free production zone in Tuzla in the far western and far eastern outskirts of Istanbul; from artistic and social project management restricted to the Taksim-Beyoğlu district to *dershanes* and foundation university campuses scattered all around the city; from the insurance/finance sector jammed into the plaza area in Maslak to call centers spread over various districts, either concentrated or scattered. Discussing the diversity of spatial experience in Istanbul also makes it possible to rethink the differences in working conditions. We have a double aim here. By posing questions about differences, we attempted to identify commonalities, intersections, collectivities and possibilities for encounters in Istanbul. Laboring worlds are located side by side yet not touching each other, commodities and spaces produced by the labor that is mobile in the city but fixed at the workplace. Which perspective do we need to choose to see in a unified manner this state of laboring bodies simultaneously intersecting with, and diverging from, one another in the city? How could we represent the differentiating unity of Istanbul from the perspective of the social sciences?[10]

---

10 Here we can propose some examples from the artistic field that can serve as an inspiration for a dialectical representation of the diversified unity called the city. The poet İlhan Berk's *Istanbul Kitabı* written in 1947 (1997, Istanbul: Adam Yayınları) seems to apply the same view of the city as film director

The panel participants' narratives show that one can identify tangible spatial, experiential and dispositional differences between differently laboring bodies. These differences, however, do not necessarily fit in with the classifications defined by mainstream economics, such as blue versus white collar, or industry versus services sector workers. When we zoom out, put the narratives side by side, and see them in a rather abstract way, we recognize the commonalities that cut across all the contributions.

DIFFERENCES/DIFFERENTIATIONS WITHIN COMMONALITIES

There are various factors that differentiate between a call center worker, a construction worker, a *dershane* instructor, an insurance agent, a culture manager, an NGO employee, an employee of a foundation university and an apparel worker in Istanbul. Among these are also different uses of the body and different "horizons of expectations,"[11] which led me to consider keeping the old dichotomy of mental labor versus manual labor in my re-

---

Alejandro González Iñárritu when describing Mexico City in *Amores Perros* (2000) and Barcelona in *Biutiful* (2010).

11 Interestingly, the term "expectation" has so far only been theorized and operationalized in mainstream economics from the start of the twentieth century. It was used to explain the psychological aspects of the investor's behavior in order to prevent chain reactions, mainly in money markets, that led to breakdowns. There is a single entry on "expectations" in the most exhaustive encyclopeadia of social sciences in the anglophone world, namely the *International Encyclopaedia of Social and Behavioural Sciences*, and it deals with the "economics of expectations" (Evans, G.W. and S. Honkapohja [2001], "Expectations, Economics of," in *International Encyclopaedia of Social and Behavioural Sciences*, ed. Neil J. Smelser and Paul B. Baltes, Oxford: Pergamon Press, pp. 5060-5067). I deem this aspect of expectations to be central to this field of work, and I aspire to produce an "anthropology of expectations in labor relations." For a philsophical analysis of the interrelations between work, labor, self-esteem, value and hope in society, see Hannah Arendt's seminal work *The Human Condition* (1958, Chicago: The University of Chicago Press).

search for a while. However, I was not sure to what extent I could use the category of "mental labor," since it tacitly implies a freedom to take initiative at work, when classifying workplaces where teachers are "stacked as if in a factory," and insurance packages are sold or calls are picked up in a mass production rhythm. I believe that a separate discussion about the discrepancy between the image of so-called white collar desk jobs, which seem to have a high social status, and the actual reality of these jobs today, needs to be pursued. As a matter of fact, the narratives of white collar participants in the panel were incredibly striking in that they show me how white collar workers intensely suffer from their working conditions in contrast to how it may seem from the outside. The stories mostly suggest that "white collar workers" are "emotionally coerced to work", as it requires a much greater emotional and financial investment to maintain the image inherited from the old social value system about the white collar, allegedly "elegant" desk jobs identified with mental labor. One of the significant surprising moments was the realization that a construction worker, moving from site to site without any expectation of job security, and hence without any anxiety about losing his job, felt himself more a "free worker" and with greater flexibility than a cultural manager. Yet the cultural manager, who is indeed expected to be nomadic and bohemian, felt limited to a narrow urban space around the Taksim district, and dependent on just a few NGOs and culture bosses in the sector.

In the realm of "labor regime/disciplining of labor," economic and emotional coercion play different roles to varying degrees, depending on whether one works at a construction site/factory or in a plaza/office. What imposes discipline/conformity on a construction worker so that he will work at a construction site, and what imposes discipline/conformity on the employee of a foundation university so that she will work on a campus, are structurally different. Here I would again consider the concept of "horizon of expectations" which gathers the interrelations between the subjectivities of workers with the hardcore realities of the workplace. Some of the participants argued that working in an office, in the services sector or as a white collar worker caused much greater alienation because the emotional pressure on the individualized self plays a primary role in the psychodynamics of working. In the panel we discussed whether the main distinction between blue and white collar workers was the difference in their wages, and agreed that the wage discrepancy should be recalculated by taking into account the expenses white collar workers must assume in order to keep up with the social image expected of them by their companies, this in addition to their household debts such as credit card expenses and private bank loans. Also blue collar workers have to keep up a social image which seems to be more imposed on them by the wider family circle than their employers.

Speaking of concrete differences in Istanbul, manual workers are much more unfairly exposed to health problems and lose their physical well-being much more directly in comparison with mental workers, since there is a higher prevalence of occupational accidents and diseases caused by intense exposure to chemicals and other factors, at factories and construction sites. Although there is no comparative research on class inequalities regarding workers' health in Turkey, what we can conclude from our panel discussions is that psychosocial occupational diseases more frequently associated with white collar work cause less harm to physical health and incur a smaller number of deaths; white collar workers have a greater life expectancy in comparison to industrial workers. This is one of the additional research agendas the panel enabled me to define. It is clearly not possible to expand on this topic theoretically and at greater length within the space of this paper. As I mentioned earlier, the aim of this inquiry is relatively modest: to roughly suggest tracks for possible research agendas by regrouping impressions.

Speaking of the differences between working practices in cool Istanbul, it would be well justified to approach the city as the accumulation, development and differentiation site of different types of capital, economic, cultural and social, as Bourdieu defines them. And the symbolic capital whose accumulated version forms the dominant image/brand of the city serves to naturalize the uneven distribution of these three types of capital.[12] With respect to differentiation and differences, white collar workers' une-

---

12   For a synthetic account of the forms of capital and how their distribution forms the field of analysis, see Bourdieu, Pierre (1986), "The forms of capital," in *Handbook of Theory and Research for the Sociology of Education*, ed. J. Richardson, New York: Greenwood, pp. 241-258. Bourdieu's disciple, Loïc Wacquant, has rigorously applied this field analysis to several phenomena of uneven distribution of capital in the cities, focusing on urban marginalization and the urban poor. See Wacquant, Loïc (2007), *Urban Outcast: A Comparative Sociology of Advanced Marginality*, Cambridge: Polity Press.

ven possession of cultural and social capital opens "scars of difference" on industrial laborers[13] who are becoming more and more estranged to Istanbul day by day, while the preponderant symbolic capital of white collar work, has also largely deteriorated and already lost most of its sparkle. We can see a parallel between this estrangement and the Environmental Plan for Istanbul, announced in 2009.[14] Despite having already been practically suspended by governmental authorities in Ankara, the plan states that the current 32% share of the industrial sector must be decreased to 20% in the medium term, revealing the plans to turn Istanbul into a finance center and "creative services city." The plan notes that the decentralization of industry is not only a spatial removal but it also corresponds to symbolic marginalization of industrial work. This is also clearly the case with the imagination of cool Istanbul, which excludes the spaces, people and symbols associated with industrial production. One of the most striking pieces of evidence for this transformation is that old, large, industrial sites are being renovated and turned into foundation university buildings, congress halls and museums. That is, the so-called culture industries are replacing the industrial cultures, landscapes, and populations of the previous period.[15]

---

13 Istanbul is represented /branded with images and discourses of white collar, "creative" plaza work. Only a brief look at the advertisement strategies of prestigious commodities like gated communities, cars, exclusive food, would suffice to witness the use of the white collar images to show workers which sector has accumulated more symbolic capital in the city.

14 See the summary of the notes to the Plan: http://www.ibb.gov.tr/tr-TR/Documents/ISTANBUL_CDP_GENEL_BILGI.pdf (accessed 24 March 2014).

15 Please note that the term "cultural industries" is mainly a product of the early 1980's and it is diametrically opposed to the Frankfurt School's analysis of the culture industry. The latter is a term coined by Theodor W. Adorno and Max Horkheimer who reflected upon the use of media on the masses to support the fascist regimes in the Interwar period. It is thus situated within a critique of commodity fetishism expanding itself upon the cultural and communicational fields in mass society. See particularly the section "The Culture Industry: Enlightenment as Mass Deception," in *Dialectics of Enlightenment. Philosophical Fragments* (2002 [1944]):, Stanford: Stanford University Press, pp. 94-137. Yet the former concept takes for granted the production of culture by the private sector, and the city that competes with its creative potentials. For a

COMMONALITIES WITHIN DIFFERENCES

The panel showed that some commonalities between workers are already crystallizing. First, we listened to countless examples illustrating how the workplaces are necessarily spatially coded in order to consolidate hierarchies. It does not matter what the workplace is or what kind of a commodity or service is produced there. This could sometimes be the team leader at the call center, a foreman at the construction site, shift boss at the factory, department director at the insurance agency, head of department or administrator at the university, project coordinator at the NGO or cultural sector. Hierarchies and promotion systems are always coded in space and bodies so that they can be used for the everyday disciplining of labor. The call center leader might have the privilege of not using headphones; the department director might have a separate office; the foreman might wear a different uniform, the shift boss might wear a small ribbon on the uniform, the project coordinator might be able to move more freely and to enter places where others are not allowed. Such spatial coding also helps to organize and canalize workers' infinite human dreams and expectations. Spatial routines are used by the workplace regime to engineer and to manage their expectations, lest they become daring, dangerous and uncanny to the workplace regime. The stories told about this subject were so abundant as to elicit a new sub-discipline for the anthropology of space and work entitled "Spatial mechanisms of expectation engineering at workplaces." This type of engineering cuts and redresses spatially unbound human dreams into spatially recognizable patterns of success, promotion and punishment at the workplace.

We have noticed that the feeling of obligation pervading the most distressed statements during the sessions is based on the idea that work corresponds to social success, and social success to successfully competing with co-workers. We can propose that separating the definition of success from the richness, commonality, endlessness of human dreams, and narrowing the definition of the co-worker to "the other," to the idea that "the one next to me is my boundary" is a major reason for serious work miseries. Having to produce things collaboratively, yet defining your occupational and social

---

brief summary, see Power, Dominic and Allen J. Scott, Allen J. (2004), *Cultural Industries and the Production of Culture*, Routledge: Oxford.

identity in competition with your co-workers constitutes a grave contradiction in itself. The latest methods in the field of business administration, mainly within the departments of operation management, have coded and polished the methods of intra-mate competition on the shop floor to increase productivity.[16]

When we started discussing working conditions, even those participants in their late 30s, with an average of 10 to 15-year-work experience, stated that, compared to ten years ago, they were now working more intensely, for longer hours and in a more unqualified manner. Except for two workers in their 20s and 50s respectively, the eight presenters said that the work they are doing is/feels less valuable, more standardized, and leaves less space to take initiatives, as compared to what they would have hoped for/expected/dreamt about in their work-lives. Some of them called this process "proletarianization" of their occupations except for the apparel and construction workers.[17] There was an agreement that work is unidentifiably fragmented for the individual worker, increasingly undermining our perception of work as a whole, an integrated process, no matter what the final product might be: an insurance package, a building, a teaching curriculum, education, a performance or a social project.

Each workplace has its own mechanisms of recruitment, hierarchization and reproduction. Some of the examples we discussed are as follows. The construction sites demand that workers work more intensely and longer hours even though the subcontractors do not pay for overtime work. The distinction between private life and working time becomes more vague as employees in the financial sector are forced to be accessible through smart phones at all times. Research activities in the field of education are spatially

---

16 See Vincent Gaulejac's (2005) pathbreaking analysis of the overarching consequences of the application of the latest methods of business administration in all spheres of life: *La société malade de la gestion: Idéologie gestionnaire, pouvoir managérial et harcèlement social*, Paris: Seuil.

17 The term used in Turkish was *işçileşme* which mainly refers to the delusion suffered by the younger generations of the educated middle class who had hoped to remain outside manual work, and to maintain their corresponding social status in society. That the white collar, office job seemed to not deliver the expected status in society any longer was one of the most common statements in the previous section dealing with differences in work lives.

outsourced from the workplace to the private space in favor of mass private education. Call center work is defined as unqualified work from the very beginning as the employers go so far as to assert that "to breath and be able to speak are the only requirements" for employment. Whereas call center business feeds off the ranks of the reserve army of labor (the unemployed in Marx's terms) and fills the same ranks in return, an ancient occupation such as teaching, which is also considered to be "the founding occupation of the Turkish Republic," is losing much prestige. This is exemplified in the case of hourly paid teachers working in schools and *dershane*s. Furthermore, there is also the more somber case of the teachers who fall victims to the great distance between their occupational expectations and reality. Their tragedies go down in history as "the stories of teachers who commit suicide waiting to be assigned to a post."[18] The panel reinforced my tentative decision to call this psychosocial state shared by all workers "work misery" (*souffrance au travail*). With this concept, I refer to being spiritually and physically badly affected by the discrepancy between what is expected of a job and what is actually experienced at work. It would not be an overestimation to claim that this relative discrepancy between expectation and perceived reality, called work misery, is shared by white and blue collar workers alike in all facets of life, in contrast to the class inequalities with respect to life expectancy and health issues I mentioned above.

In all the narratives, the participants referred or alluded to the metaphors of spatial confinement and prison in order to express the limitations in the workplace. "The cultural life jammed around Taksim;" "the run-

---

18 Ataması Yapılmayan Öğretmenler Platformu (AYÖP) defends the rights of the graduates of the education faculties waiting to be assigned a post by the Turkish Ministry of Education. In 2011, around 230 thousand teachers took the central exam for teachers (KPSS), although only 27 thousand were assigned a job. So far 30 suicides among teachers who were not placed have been found to be motivated by disillusionment when faced with permanent unemployment and precarity, despite their high qualifications. For the KPSS (Kamu Personeli Seçme Sınavı/Exam for Selecting Personnel for the Public Sector) suicides and the political-economic background of teacher assignments see Semiz, Duygu (2013), "Öğretmenlerde Meslek Hastalıkları ve Sınav İntiharları," *Eğitim Bilim Toplum* 11 (41), pp. 101-110 (special issue on job precarity and worker's health and safety).

down shanties where mostly migrant and nomadic construction workers are enclosed;" "the plazas with shiny faces, out of which white collar workers rush at the end of the work day, just like primary school pupils running into the school garden at breaks as soon as the bells ring;" "foundation university campuses scarily 'in the middle of nowhere' where no ambulances are close enough to help if anything happens;" free production zones which are marketed with the slogan "you have now entered the EU" but are managed through nothing other than a typical factory control regime; "bodies stuck in chairs," not even free to go to the toilet whenever they want, "one ear submitted to the customer, the other ear submitted to the team leader." Our descriptions were as intense and passionate as the work miseries experienced. Apparently, the workers of Istanbul experience the city in enclosed workspaces and do not want to hear much about work once they leave the workplace. It might be necessary to start another investigation about the objective and subjective reasons why workers rush to shopping malls or prefer to sit in front of the television during the time they reproduce their labor power, why they generate other socio-spatial (self-)confinements with their bodies, at home and in public spaces.

After discussing this feeling of confinement and being continuously in competition with one's co-workers, many anecdotes were told, and reasons given about why it is so difficult to establish concrete solidarity patterns outside the reach of the spatial and social classification mechanisms of the system mentioned above. The participants of the panel agreed on the impact of the objective obstacles created by the state and the employers against labor-based solidarity actions: the notary and national threshold which prevail for the trade unions to have the right to collective bargaining with the employer, the difficulty of pursuing one's legal rights after being laid off etc. Moreover, one of the most important contributions of the panel was shedding light on the subjective obstacles to workers' solidarity. These obstacles seem to become even more reinforced in step with their internalization, as a consequence of the way micropower relations function on the shop floor.

Another important discussion was about how furious the acts of solidarity and microrevolts against spatial/temporal arrangements of the workplace regime can become, and how anger wells up and bursts. In this framework, the participants also cited hierarchical stratification according to age differences as a subjective difficulty, in addition to class distinctions in the workplace. The panel made clear that in each workplace and line of business, there was some gerontocratic oppression. This usually means that the latecomers to a sector are exposed to multiple forms of exploitation as they work under the worst conditions and, the burden of the workplace is on their shoulders. Whether it be academia, the financial sector, a factory, or culture and the arts, newcomers to a workplace must begin work in a much more precarious manner. In contrast, the older staff members usually cling to their small or large privileges. They tend to hang on to these privileges and practice a conformist and oppressive policy against younger workers. Although these privileges are not based on the nature of the work done, the older employees attempt to make the great distance between the working conditions of the two generations look more natural. For example, the graduate students who are at best integrated as part-time instructors or teaching assistants in academia carry the brunt of the teaching load in order to free the higher echelons of the academic staff from "non-prestigious" work, and mostly have no real hope of finding a stable academic position because of the increasing lack of tenured posts.

The age difference is also connected with masculine domination in the workplace, as mentioned during the panel. Gerontocracy has got a gender. During the panel, it became clear that masculine domination is even prevalent in the fields of culture and the arts, and social project management, which seemingly allow more freedom in terms of the expression of individual sexual orientation than other sectors. In addition, it was striking to notice that what defines and motivates the construction business and the purely masculine space of the construction site is not the relational tension between gender roles, but rather the construction workers' unilateral masculine dreams to "marry a girl of their choice" without interference from their families in their hometowns.

The panel participants agreed that waiting for a union to organize workplaces was "as if waiting for Godot" or choosing one of the existing unions in Istanbul would not be enough to overcome the problems with working conditions and labor organization. It became clear that solidarity and organization were not coming to town by themselves! We touched upon the importance of micro-organizations which are established in spite of all the objective and subjective obstacles, or perhaps exactly because of them, and in particular thanks to the work miseries uniting all the workers. Such micro-organizations, usually called platforms, networks, or initiatives, are formed as workers from or within specific workplaces share their experiences, which also comprise "channels of communication and friendly local chat" to overcome spatial and social isolation and competition at work.

Another commonality mentioned in the sessions was about the centralization and financialization of the economic capital that has evolved into a conglomerate-like structure investing in many sectors simultaneously. This process entails a transformation of the city in order to harmonize working conditions inside the networks that cannot be seen with the naked eye, but are revealed by large corruption scandals.[19] There are numerous examples such as construction companies establishing foundation universities, hospital chains getting into the construction business, big financial actors making investments in the culture and arts sector, etc. In other words, what is in question is a re-scaling and geographical/sectoral scattering of capital, and that the traditional trade union structures cannot live up to the fast and constantly changing socio-spatial organization of economic capital. It would be too naive to ignore that this affects working conditions negatively, exercising social dumping and establishing similar workplace regimes and remunerations at the detriment of the labor force. When a cost-saving strategy is applied to a sector, another sector copies these strategies. The labor subcontracting system was first applied to construction work, then to the production sector, and then slightly adapted by the health and education sectors. The flexibilization methods are copied and pasted, and the conglomerate structure of the economic capital accelerates the transfer of cost-savings and labor-disciplining knowledge from one sector to the other at the detriment of the worker's welfare.

Therefore, if we had a chance a century later from now, to look at the work relations of our times and their spatial organizations, there would be

---

19 For examples, see the "Networks of Dispossession" Project: http://mulksuzles tirme.org/index_en.html (accessed 5 May 2014). This is a collective effort to compile data to map the relationship between capital and direct political power in urban transformation in Turkey. The project is the product of a platform comprising digital artists, urban sociologists, journalists, and was formed during the Gezi uprisings in Taksim, June 2013. Their website is an interactive mapping of the organic relations between the biggest companies in different sectors, the bureaucracy, media and interest groups feeding the construction sector in Turkey.

two institutional structures and metaphors which all prospective researchers would have to define preliminarily. The first is "subcontractor," the second one is "tender." Doesn't that also suggest what is in common among social and cultural projects acquired through applications, construction contracts, paid (substitute) teaching, hourly paid lecturing at a university, outsourced apparel factories, and outsourced communication and insurance services? They all work through the mechanisms, institutional structures and metaphors of outsourcing. Subcontractor is the actor and tender is the technique of the outsourcing process. It seems that political, social and economic networks created by outsourcing (and tender) relations also make the conditions of various lines of business and work places considerably resemble each other in the city.

COOL WORKERS VS. BRANDERS OF SOLIDARITY

This chapter records the important points raised in a rich panel session where eight residents of Istanbul described decades of working experience. In the preparatory meeting before the panel, we posed the following preliminary questions: How far does the imagination of "cool Istanbul" and "the other Istanbul" correspond to our working conditions and feelings associated with work? Can we see the concrete products of our labor in these images? Does "cool Istanbul" provide us with the symbolic antennas that can make us be seen in our productive practices as well as our practices as consumers of all types of commodities produced by others? The panel did not answer these questions fully but rather attempted to sow the seeds.

Before I conclude, there is one more question I would like to pose to begin a dialogue with the goals of the Cool Istanbul research project. There is a need, even urgency to creating labor-based, horizontal collectivities outside urban enclosures. However, is there anything cool or joyful about the solidarity we establish to have a say about our working conditions, and to protect our dignity/selves/health beyond normative principle? I would tentatively argue, yes. The mainstream, the system is never cool. Cool is what is alternative, critical, dissident, rebellious, uncommon, spontaneous, unique, and that which cannot be reproduced like a commodity. Yet, the twentieth century has witnessed processes of appropriation of critical contents that blossomed within an atmosphere of social exclusion[20] by the culture industry. Originally this cool, dissident content flourished in the urban peripheries since there was no space for it in the central places. It is true that solidarity and organizing is cool as long as it has a lasting and effective dissident character, proposing and trying to embody an alternative temporal/spatial/bodily organization. But I feel the real issue is to refuse to allow the high culture appropriations that deprive solidarity of vital force and content by trying to sell a superficial shell of it, and to avoid creating and identifying cool heroes and geniuses. Persistent and transformative dissidence in solidarity is only formed in collectivities, which in turn are formed by workers of solidarity and not of branders of solidarity. This is because the urban collective is originally based on the use value of solidarity which necessarily. The collective would lose its reason for being if the exchange value of solidarity replaced its use value, if solidarity were turned into a scarce commodity exchanged in the market and reproduced through its cool images.

Translated from Turkish to English by Funda Özokçu.

---

20 The histories of how, where and when blues, jazz, tango, rembetiko or Turkish arabesque developed originally as "acts of resistance" interrelate organically with social exclusion, exposure to marginalization and symbolic violence. For the social genealogy of tango, see Castro, Donald S. (1991), *The Argentine Tango As Social History, 1880-1955: The Soul of the People*, New York: Edwin Mellen. For rembetiko see Petropoulos, Elias (2000), *Songs of the Greek Underworld: The Rebetika Tradition*, London: Saqi Books. For Istanbul, one can look at the slow but consistent gentrification of the arabesque in music and film which originally served as a musical intermediary expressing the shock of the migrants exposed to symbolic violence in metropolises beginning with the 1950s. See Özbek, Meral (1991), *Popüler Kültür ve Orhan Gencebay Arabeski*, Istanbul: İletişim. For an analysis of "gentrification of arabesque" see Tekelioğlu, Orhan (2010), "Arabesk dönmüyor, soylulaşıyor!" *Radikal*, 11.07.2010 (http://www.radikal.com.tr/radikal2/arabesk_donmuyor_soylulasiyor-1007342, accessed 24 March 2014). In this volume Derya Özkan also touches upon the ways in which cultural production, which is originally critical, dissident, uncommon, is subjected to high culture appropriations and thus its political criticism domesticated.

Part II
Visual Imaginations of Cool Istanbul

HOT SUITES

No : 7 →

From Wim Wender's Lisbon to Fatih Akın's Istanbul
Producing the Cool City in Film[1]

ÖZLEM KÖKSAL

In 1994, German filmmaker Wim Wenders made a film about Lisbon called *Lisbon Story*. The film was commissioned by the City of Lisbon to promote the city when it was selected as the Cultural Capital of Europe in 1994. The film looks at Lisbon through music in particular, and through the sounds of the city in general. Although not commissioned by any organization, in 2005 Fatih Akın made a similar film about Istanbul called *Crossing the Bridge*. The film coincided with rising tourist interest in Istanbul, as well as with its selection as the Cultural Capital of Europe for 2010, as announced in 2006. Akın's film took a similar approach to Wenders, and imagined the city as a multicultural place with diverse sounds. This chapter looks at these two films, and compares their approach to the city. It also examines their

---

1 This article is based on a lecture I gave with Luis Trindade, the chair of the World Cinema MA program at Birkbeck College, University of London, as part of a course he taught in 2011. I would like to thank him for initiating the idea for the lecture, and for the discussions that took place prior to and during the lecture. I would also like to thank the organizers and the participants of the conference "Cool Istanbul: Urban Enclosures and Resistances." In particular, I thank İpek Türeli for her comments on an earlier version of this paper. İpek Çelik also read various versions of this text and provided me with comments and criticism for which I am grateful.

Photograph: Derya Özkan

potential impact on the imagination and perception of their respective cities, with particular focus on Istanbul.

The two films share many common elements. Having already directed several critically acclaimed films, Wenders had been awarded the Grand Prix at the Cannes Film Festival before making *Lisbon Story*. Similarly, while making *Crossing the Bridge*, Fatih Akın was well on his way to becoming a star on the international festival circuit, as well as in Germany and Turkey, and had won the Golden Bear for his *Gegen Die Wand/Head-on* (2004). Both Wenders' *Lisbon Story* and Akın's *Crossing the Bridge* are about exploring their respective cities through music and sound, trying to find a portal into their supposedly secret/hidden soul. In other words, what we have are two award winning directors with their own distinctive styles, both critically acclaimed and sought after in festival circuits, and both dealing with two "cool cities."

Although elusive, "cool" is a word used in relation to both cities in the media. A recent piece on CNN International's website designated Lisbon as "probably the coolest city in Europe."[2] Similarly, as Derya Özkan outlines in her chapter in this volume, global media within the last decade has highlighted Istanbul as a cool city with a vibrant culture and nightlife. This conceptualization undeniably creates attraction by presenting the city as a source of numerous opportunities for visitors and investors alike. Hence, the concept of cool, although loaded and simultaneously empty, or perhaps because it is loaded and empty at the same time, brings to mind an image of its referent. Films can contribute to the creation of that image by reciprocally creating and reproducing how a city is perceived. As I will argue below, both films produce a particular imagination of coolness in relation to these cities, and in so doing, dwell on nostalgic representations: Lisbon as a dreamy, historical city frozen in time, Istanbul as a buzzing and trendy city that bridges cultures.

Before examining these films closely, I would like to mention two other concepts that are as elusive as the concept of cool: world cinema and world music. Although the categories of "world music" and "world cinema" connote different things depending on the context of their use, there is an inevi-

---

2   Dunlop, Fiona, "7 reasons Lisbon could be Europe's coolest city," *CNN International*, 26 January 2014 (http://edition.cnn.com/2014/01/25/travel/lisbon-coolest-city, accessed 9 April 2014).

table marketing effort interwoven with the coining and usage of these terms. Writing on world music, Martin Stokes notes that the term dates from 1987, when executives of a record company in London wanted to find ways to market the currently circulating commercial recordings to consumers in Britain.³ The term was picked up by the music press in the west and is often used in relation to music influenced by non-western musical traditions.

The use of world cinema as a classification is also connected to the global marketing of cultures. Although the term is often used critically to contrast Hollywood with other national cinemas, and can be a useful conception in that sense, it is also, and more often, used as with world music, i.e. as "a tidy agglomeration that suits the marketing and governing principles of major multinational industrial concerns but deracinates the cultural histories and conflicts that makes possible its very components."⁴ Hence the conception of both world cinema and world music is interwoven with the dynamics of the global economy.⁵ On the one hand, they both connote authenticity, positioned as differing from the dominant forms of western popular music or Hollywood cinema. On the other, they form a portmanteau concept where what is included or excluded is not fixed, instead changing not only in time but also according to the approach and location.

Both *Lisbon Story* and *Crossing the Bridge* are considered examples of world cinema outside of their countries of origin, and the music used in these films as world music. Wenders focuses on one particular genre of music, fado, performed by the modern fado band Madredeus. Fado emerged in the streets of Lisbon in the nineteenth century, and "became Portugal's 'national' music in the twentieth."⁶ Although Madredeus were

---

3   Stokes, Martin (2006), "Music and the Global Order," *Annual Review of Anthropology* 33, p. 52.
4   Miller, Toby (2005), "Preface," in *Traditions in World Cinemas*, ed. Badley, Linda, Barton, R. Barton and Steven Jay Schneider, New Jersey: Rutgers University Press, p. xi.
5   For a discussion of world music in relation to Istanbul's music scene, see Değirmenci, Koray (2013), *Creating Global Music in Turkey*, Lanham: Lexington Books.
6   Elliot, Richard (2010), *Fado and the Place of Longing: Loss, Memory and the City*, Surrey: Ashgate, p. 128.

well known at the time, the film exposed them to an even wider audience. Richard Elliot writes that "outside of Portugal, the group became one of the first Portuguese acts—and certainly the first 'non-traditional' act—to be included in the newly formed 'world music' category, gaining them further exposure via the emerging world music media."[7]

Akın's film, on the other hand, includes numerous musicians and musical genres, opening with a composition by Mercan Dede who is known for his electronic take on Sufi music. The director then introduces other musical genres, and ends the film with an oriental version of Madonna's "Music" as sung by Eurovision winner Sertap Erener. Unsurprisingly, the soundtrack for the film was released as a CD by the world music label Doublemoon, one of the prominent world music labels in Turkey. In addition, both directors deal with world cities en route to becoming European Cultural Capitals, hence the context for the films' production and release are interwoven with preparations in these cities for that event. Nevertheless, these films are neither mere marketing products intended exclusively to market the city, nor can they be considered completely detached from the images these cities hold.[8]

Since films about cities contribute to the perception of those cities, it is inevitable that they should often be discussed in those terms as well. Wenders, for instance, in response to a question about whether he is aware of anyone wanting to visit Lisbon after seeing his film, says: "I don't want to brag, but I know of hundreds of people over the years who said they went to see the city because of the film."[9] What is noteworthy here is the approach that sees the film's success in connection to its contribution to the marketing of the city. In other words, while Wenders did not create the film with the aim of increasing the number of tourists visiting Lisbon, it became one of the ways in which its success is measured. Although there is nothing

---

7   Ibid, p.1.
8   Although Wenders' film was commissioned by the City of Lisbon, Wenders had artistic freedom while making the film, and the film circulates as "a film by Wim Wenders." As such the grounds for comparison are not contaminated by the fact that one of these films was commissioned.
9   Wenders, Wim (2003), "These Songs Were My Script—'Lisbon Story' revisited," (http://www.wim-wenders.com/news_reel/2003/sept-interview-lisbon.htm, accessed 9 April 2014).

wrong with a film generating tourist interest in a place, it is worth considering why the most immediate question is one about tourist interest, which then becomes an important parameter against which to measure the film's success. In contrast, much less is said about how locals engage with such films, which in return can be seen as an indication of the fact that these films are predominantly imagined for outsiders. "Outsiders" here does not necessarily mean foreigners, but a potential target audience whose knowledge of the city is limited and to whom the image will be sold.

Hence, there is an inescapable commodification of cities in and by films like *Lisbon Story* and *Crossing the Bridge*. Deniz Göktürk, writing on the subject, notes that "commodification of places relies on a recognizable uniqueness while, paradoxically, erasing specificity in the spread and expanse of tradable resemblances."[10] This unique image must be recognizable enough to not alienate, yet different enough to attract. How, then, do these films take part in the commodification of their respective cities?

LISBON STORY: A FROZEN CITY

Wenders, at the time of making the *Lisbon Story*, was an established director, having already directed critically acclaimed films such as *Paris Texas* (1984) and *Wings of Desire* (1987). When he was approached by the City of Lisbon to make a film about Lisbon as part of the efforts to celebrate Lisbon's selection as the Cultural Capital of Europe in 1994, he opted to not make a documentary about the city, although he wanted to use it as the main character.[11] While he was preparing for the film, he met Madredeus and decided to include them as part of the story of Lisbon. The band at the time happened to have twelve unpublished songs about Lisbon, which Wenders used as his script.[12] The film begins with Philip Winter (Rudiger Vogler), a sound engineer, receiving a letter from his old friend Friedrich, a film director, inviting Philip to Lisbon to make a film about/in the city. In

---

10 Göktürk, Deniz (2010), "Projecting Polyphony: Moving Images, Travelling Sounds," in *Orienting Istanbul: Capital of Europe*, ed. Göktürk, Deniz, Soysal, Levent and Ipek Türeli, New York: Routledge, p. 180.
11 Wenders (2003), "These Songs Were My Script."
12 Ibid.

Lisbon, while waiting for his friend to appear, Philip explores the city and starts recording the sounds of the city. Following his encounter with the members of the band Madredeus, who happen to reside in the same building, he starts visiting them often, listening to their rehearsals. It is through Philip's walks in the city and Madredeus' music that the audience discovers Lisbon.

Wenders, in *Lisbon Story*, treats the city as a frozen temporality which inevitably forces the director to deal with a frozen city. With his camera seemingly wandering deep into the city, the director seeks to capture its essence. This essence, the "mythical uncontaminated space,"[13] is found in Alfama, where most of the film takes place. Alfama is one of the oldest, and possibly the most touristy neighborhoods in Lisbon. Unlike other areas, it was fortunate to survive the famous earthquake of 1755. The area provides historic old buildings and narrow streets for the camera; it is a picturesque neighborhood where time seems to stand still. Wenders' decision to limit his representation of Lisbon predominantly to Alfama produces a nostalgic representation of the city.

It is hard to tell how much of Wenders' own experience and preconceptions of the city influenced the representation of Lisbon in the film, and how much of this representation was dictated by the city itself. Lisbon, according to the director, appeared to be a "dreamy" city in disbelief "that it was actually part of Europe. Somehow it had turned its back to the continent and was looking over the ocean as if it had hopes to find its long lost splendor there again."[14] In other words, although Wenders does not clarify whether he is referring to the Portuguese colonial past when he mentions a "long lost splendour," this assumed loss is the dominant feeling in the film. It is more than likely that Wenders' belief that he found something recognizably unique in Alfama shaped his vision of the city.

This feeling of nostalgia produced about the city in the image track is further enhanced with the use of fado as the soundtrack, since fado is "known for its strong emphasis on loss, memory and nostalgia within its song texts."[15] According to Elliot:

---

13   Chambers, Iain (2002), *Migrancy, Culture, Identity*, London: Routledge, p. 72.
14   Wenders (2003), "These Songs Were My Script."
15   Elliot (2010), *Fado and the Place of Longing*, p. 1.

One of the main lyrical themes of fado is the city itself, particularly those areas most associated with the music's origin such as Alfama [...] A mythology of place is summed up in fado song texts that attempts to trace the remembered and imagined city of the past via the poetics of haunting. At the same time, certain locales of the physical city present themselves as stages in a museum of song, offering up haunted melodies of a sonic past that serve to assert the city's identity. City and song, bear witness to each other.[16]

What is more, one of the qualities associated with fado is *saudade,* a Portuguese word often considered untranslatable to other languages. In his book on fado, Richard Elliot gives a detailed account of what the word means and the story behind its untranslatable status.[17] Loosely referring to sorrow and loss (or sorrow of loss) the discussion on *saudade* is very much reminiscent of Orhan Pamuk's discussion of the Turkish word *hüzün* as the dominant feeling in Istanbul. Pamuk also claims that the word has no corresponding term in other languages, hence the Turkish word *hüzün* is used in the English translation.[18] However, as Elliot also quotes in his book in relation to the untranslatable status of *saudade,* Svetlana Boym points out that there is a "grammar of nostalgia" in these discussions of untranslatability. According to Boym,

while each term preserves the specific rhythms of the language, one is struck by the fact that all these untranslatable words are in fact synonyms; and all share the desire for untranslatability, the longing for uniqueness. While the details and flavors differ, the grammar of romantic nostalgias all over the world is quite similar. "I long therefore I am" became the romantic motto.[19]

Wenders nevertheless gives a glimpse of the expanding city of Lisbon towards the end of the film, albeit briefly. The camera goes outside of Al-

---

16   Ibid, p. 1-2.
17   For a discussion of the concept and its place in fado see Elliot (2010), *Fado and the Place of Longing*, pp. 27-32.
18   Pamuk, Orhan. (2005), *Istanbul:Memories of a City*, London: Faber & Faber, p. 116.
19   Boym, Svetlana (2001), *The Future of Nostalgia*, New York: Basic Books, p. 13.

fama and shows modern buildings. Rather than embracing the relatively new part of the city and perhaps seeing its older and newer parts, Wenders makes the modern buildings look like a disease that the city is battling. Furthermore, Wenders captures only the locals in Alfama, and excludes the crowds of tourists who would normally populate the neighborhood. This then helps the director to create the Lisbon he has in mind: a dreamy city "looking over the ocean as if it had hopes to find its long lost splendor there again." Wenders' imagination and the representation of the place are triggered by a feeling of loss, in Christine Boyer's words a loss of "continuum of traditional experience and remembrance in spatial forms."[20] Boyer, in reference to Walter Benjamin and his discussion of the loss of real experiences in modern city life, argues that because of this lack, this lack of continuity, we turn to synthetic and unnatural representations of "frozen city landscapes where memory had fallen asleep."[21]

Benjamin, in his writings, talks about the changes modern life, particularly city life, has brought with it. According to Benjamin, the modern world bombards us with information and images that subjects us to a series of shocks. This is unlike the experience Benjamin values (*Erfahrung*), best exemplified in the practice of old storytellers who "tell from experience."[22] As they pass on a given experience, the activity of storytelling creates continuity between the past and the present. In the modern world, storytelling has been replaced by information, creating an isolated experience (*Erlebnis*) not emerging within a continuum. The shocks that modern life creates are registered as isolated experiences. Boyer writes: "Consequently the continuum of traditional experience and remembrance embedded in spatial forms, once thought to be the ordering structure of the city and the generating device for memory was impoverished beyond recognition."[23]

The feeling of loss produced by Wenders' film about the city is coupled with the self-reflexive but nostalgic take on early cinema: the idea that contingency can be captured. The discussions on cinema and contingency

---

20 Boyer, Christine (1994), *The City of Collective Memory*, Massachusetts: MIT Press, p. 23.
21 Ibid., p. 24.
22 Benjamin, Walter (2007 [1969]), *Illuminations*, New York: Schocken Books, p. 87.
23 Boyer (1994), *The City of Collective Memory*, pp. 23-24.

with the larger picture these cities are desired/imagined as belonging to, dwelling on nostalgic representations.

To reiterate the earlier discussion, although the commodification of places relies on reproducing unique aspects of those places, it also needs to foreground similarities to the larger picture these cities are imagined as belonging. In the context of these two cities and these particular films, the larger picture seems to be Europe. In Lisbon's case, what is unique is the cultural (in this specific case musical) and historical (Alfama) elements found in the city. In Istanbul's case, the unique element is the city's eclectic culture, exemplified in music thought of as representative of the city. From electronic sufi music to Anatolian rock, one leaves the movie theatre with the impression that Istanbul's geographical in-betweenness finds its reflection in its music as well. This in-betweenness is produced over and over in the image of the bridge used as a metaphor for the city's historic and cultural heritage.

Hence, although the bridge metaphor is used heavily in relation to Istanbul, the similarities between the approaches and imaginations of the two cities, coincidently by directors coming from the German filmmaking tradition, might stem from an additional anxiety these cities produce, that of being in-between. Lisbon, although less so compared to Istanbul, is also often referred to as bridge between cultures, in this case between Africa and Europe.[46] This anxiety is often overcome by turning the physical non-place (the bridge) into a political and social place. Such elusive, difficult-to-pin-down understanding of the position of these cities in the cultural map can also be connected to their image as cool cities. The meaning of the concept of cool can range from calmness to being in fashion, from restraint to attractiveness, and it seems to me that visual representation of these cities, one that plays on their in-between status, is not coincidental but one that fits well into the elusive quality of the word "cool."

---

46 Rosa Williams, for instance, gives a few examples of how the language of the cultural bridge circulates in relation to Lisbon. See Williams, Rosa (2013), "Luso-African Intimacies: Conceptions of National and Transnational Community," in *Imperial Migrations*, ed. Eric Mories-Genoud and Michael Cahen, New York: Palgrave, p. 279-280.

Özge's debut *Men On the Bridge* (2009). The film focuses on three young men living in the suburbs and struggling to make a living in Istanbul. The main connection between these otherwise unrelated people is that they all "work" on the bridge: a *dolmuş* (shared-taxi) driver who crosses the bridge dozens of times every day as part of his route, a traffic policeman who works on the bridge, and an unemployed teenager who takes temporary jobs, including selling flowers to the drivers in their cars stuck in traffic on the bridge. Except for the policeman, they all play themselves, and Özge follows them, documenting their lives.

Lacking the typically reproduced views of Istanbul and the bridge, Özge treats the bridge predominantly as what it is: a steel construction allowing transportation from one end to the other. In other words, the director not only does not reproduce breathtaking views of Istanbul, but she also does not necessarily dwell on the fact that what is being crossed is a bridge connecting two continents, as is often highlighted with regards to the bridge and Istanbul's position. The bridge is the main character in Özge's film. It is cast in a role that is different from those it was previously given. Like the other characters, it acts as itself, as a massive steel construction often hosting heavy traffic, and not as a metaphor for the country's assumed historical position.

FAMILIAR OR UNIQUE?
COOL CITIES AND GLOBAL ECONOMY

Cities and their representations cannot be conceived of as separate from the global economy. Cultural life inevitably goes hand in hand with the perception of cities, and this includes cultural products produced in, and about them. This chapter, although focused on Istanbul and its imagination, compared two films, and through those films, representations of two cities: Lisbon and Istanbul. Despite the ten-year gap between the making of these films, neither the context in which they were made nor their approaches to these cities are fundamentally different. That is to say while both films focus on different aspects of their cities (*Lisbon Story* on Lisbon's place in European cultural heritage, *Crossing the Bridge* on Istanbul's eclectic culture that merges Europe and Asia) they end up highlighting similarities

time."[43] As such, the bridge metaphor for Turkey's geographical, political and cultural context projects this nostalgic idea about the country's imagined role in the world as a bridge between cultures. As Meltem Ahıska notes:

> Turkey, which has been labeled by both outsiders and insiders as a bridge between the East and the West, has an ambivalent relation not only to the geographical sites of the East and the West, but also to their temporal signification: namely, backwardness and progress. Turkey has been trying to cross the bridge between the East and the West for more than a hundred years now, with a self-conscious anxiety that it is arrested in time and space by the bridge itself. In other words, the meaning of the present has a mythical core that has persisted over years and which remains as a source of frustration and threat, and as a symptom of internalized inferiority.[44]

As Ahıska insightfully diagnoses, the bridge as a metaphor includes decades long anxieties arrested in time and space. One way to overcome this anxiety (albeit temporarily), as Boym suggests, is to produce nostalgic imaginations, an image that finds comfort somewhere in the past or in the future where uncertainties do not enter. A recent and almost literal illustration of such anxiety over what Turkey is and where it wants to be, took place when the famous golf player Tiger Woods came to Turkey in November 2013 for the opening ceremony of a Golf tournament in Antalya (southern Turkey). He hit the ball, the symbolic opening hit of the tournament, in Istanbul, over the Bosporus Bridge, which was closed to traffic on the day of the event. The ball was reportedly hit from the east towards the west. According to the *Hürriyet Daily,* Woods "became the first golfer to hit balls from East to West on the bridge that separates the continents."[45]

However, this is not to say that there is a complete lack of critical approaches to the bridge metaphor. An example of this in cinema is Aslı

---

43 Ibid, p.13.
44 Ahıska, Meltem (2003), "Occidentalism: The Historical Fantasy of the Modern," *The South Atlantic Quarterly* 102 (2-3), pp. 351-379, p. 353.
45 Hurriet Daily News, "Woods hits balls from Asia to Europe on Istanbul's Bosphorus Bridge", 4 November 2013, http://www.hurriyetdailynews.com/Istanbuls-bosphorus-bridge-to-close-for-one-hour-today-for-woods-golfshow.aspx?pageID=238&nID=57380&NewsCatID=341 (accessed 9 April 2014).

itself, was capturing movement in surprising ways. There were countless shots from cameras recording inside moving vehicles, mostly trains. Early filmmakers also tried mounting their cameras on trains, capturing their surroundings in motion, thus rendering some of the earliest examples of the tracking shot. This was the dominant interest until 1906-1907, when narrative cinema became the dominant form. However, "the cinema of attraction does not disappear with the dominance of narrative, but rather goes underground, both into certain avant-garde practices and as a component of narrative film."[41] The extensive use of aerial shots in a narrative film, then, can be seen as a similar fascination, as the cinema of attraction. In this way, the camera is able to capture motion in every possible direction, providing unfamiliar perspectives on familiar locations. *Magic Carpet Ride* uses aerial shots with a camera that flies over the city, not as a plane but as a bird: it goes up and down, starting from above, moving towards the ground, going from an overview image to a close up in one continuous shot. In other words, the camera in *Magic Carpet Ride* is not only an "omniscient eye" that "enabl[es] the spectator to master the city," as Bayrakdar and Akçalı rightly point out, but it also works on the level of sheer attraction, similar to Tom Gunning's argument in relation to early cinema.

What is more, a good proportion of the shots where the camera flies over Istanbul include the bridge, as well as the Bosporus. Recently, and not surprisingly, the bridge was used in Turkey's bid for the 2020 Olympic games. In addition to the heavy use of the bridge in commercial material, particularly in films prepared for commercial purposes, the slogan of the marketing effort "Bridge Together" also played on the concept of bridge, reflecting a certain nostalgic imagination of Istanbul as a bridge between cultures. Although nostalgia is generally conceived of as a longing for a specific place, it is in fact a yearning for a specific time, or perhaps a specific type of existence in that specific time which, according to Boym, is the result of "a new understanding of time and space."[42] This is also the paradox of nostalgia: its object is somewhere in the past, or a lost opportunity in the future, but is achievable in neither case. It depends, like progress, on "the modern conception of unrepeatable and irreversible

---

41 Gunning, Tom (1986) "Cinema of Attractions, Early film, Its Spectator and the Avant-Garde," *Wide Angle* 8 (3-4), p. 64.
42 Boym (2001), *The Future of Nostalgia*, pp.11.

marketing and sales product" and "your ticket to the film also buys you a ride over the city".[38]

Aerial vision has long fascinated humankind, and mechanical reproductions of aerial images have been discussed since they first became available, in particular their use in architecture and urban planning. They were famously praised by Le Corbusier, and opposed by the developing theory of urbanism.[39] Although they provide information that our view from the ground cannot register, they do so not in addition to what the ground vision provides but often at the expense of it. The fascination with aerial vision may lead to fetishizing views of cities and structures.[40] The use of areal images in film is different from that provided by the still images of aerial photographs, mainly because the movement available to cinematic reproduction makes a very important addition: the ability to move with the camera allows the image to juxtapose both ground and aerial views. The camera can provide aerial and ground views in isolation, as well as in relation to each other. It can even merge them when moving from one to the other. Aerial shots can serve various narrative purposes depending on how they are used. They can be used as establishing shots, or they can provide a view to spectators, a view that is not available to the diegetic characters. As was discussed above, in *Crossing the Bridge,* the purpose of the aerial shots is mainly limited to establishing the totalizing view of the city, hence providing a better grip of the geography to the audience. In *Magic Carpet Ride*, however, this fascination is taken to an extreme, reminiscent of the fascination with movement itself in early cinema.

Cinema in its early days was predominantly interested with fascinating the audience. Writing on early cinema, Tom Gunning points out that early cinema was interested in attractions, which Gunning called "cinema of attractions." One of these, in addition to film itself being the fascination

---

38 Bayrakdar, Deniz and Elif Akçalı (2010), "Istanbul Convertible: A Magic Carpet Ride through Genres," in *Orienting Istanbul: Capital of Europe,* ed. Göktürk, Deniz, Soysal, Levent and Ipek Türeli, New York: Routledge, p. 169.

39 Vidler, Anthony (2003), "Photourbanism: Planning the City from Above and from Below," in *A Companion to the City,* ed. Gary Bridge and Sophie Watson, Oxford: Blackwell, pp. 35-45.

40 See: Hecker, Tim (2010), "The Slum Pastoral: Helicopter Visuality and Koolhaas's Lagos," *Space and Culture* 13 (3), pp. 256-269.

and Asia, and between antiquity and the present day."[36] The film was made six years before the first bridge opened and three years before construction begun.[37] Hence although at that point the metaphor lacked its ultimate signifier, it was nevertheless used when referring to Turkey.

OTHER APPROACHES TO THE BRIDGE AND NOSTALGIA

Among the countless films that use the image and metaphor of the bridge exhaustively, I will mention two here by way of illustration: Yılmaz Erdoğan's *Organize İşler/Magic Carpet Ride* (2005) and Aslı Özge's *Men On the Bridge* (2009).

The male protagonist of the *Magic Carpet Ride* is the leader of a petit-crime gang that engages in various types of criminal activities, ranging from stealing cars to fraud. The female protagonist, on the other hand, is a well-educated woman whose father recently won a cash-price for a book he wrote about Turkey and the European Union. Between these worlds is another character, a failed comedian in a Superman costume, who becomes involved with the gang and falls in love with the girl. What makes the film stand out, despite the predictable plot line based on tension between two different worlds (that of the gang and the upper middle class family), is its excessive use of aerial imagery. In total, nearly ten minutes of the film consists of aerial shots of Istanbul, done with a heli-cam flying continuously over the city. Most do not serve the narrative, and are there only to fascinate the audience, making a spectacle of Istanbul. According to Deniz Bayrakdar and Elif Akçalı, in *Magic Carpet Ride* Istanbul appears as "a

---

36   BFI, "Turkey—The Bridge (1966)" (http://explore.bfi.org.uk/4ce2b6c7eb4d5, accessed 9 April 2014).

37   There is very little available on the film and its content. The British Film Institute's national archive holds a copy of the film, but upon request to view it responded that the copy was kept for preservation purposes only, and is not available for viewing as it is the only copy. However, they noted, it may become accessible in the future when/if a viewing copy is made.

problematic. The term always implies a gap, a gap to be bridged, and hence carries a complicated relationship. Although Akın allows the opinions of those who ridicule the idea of bridging cultures to be heard in the film, he nevertheless ends up emphasizing the idea, hence reproducing it. In addition to the emphasis placed on the bridge in the title, there are also repeated points made about Turkey's position between the east and the west, and Turkey's position as a bridge between cultures in the actual film itself.

Although the bridge over the Bosphorous is the most used site when representing Istanbul, and perhaps the most loaded visual element, it is not the only location. There are a number of other recognizable places often used in films. However, the choice of location as representative of Istanbul differs not so much according to the genre but according to who is making the film. For filmmakers in Turkey, one of the iconic images as an entry point to the city was long provided by Haydarpaşa train station. However, this has not been the choice location for western filmmakers. Instead, they have often used the Galata Bridge, which spans not the Bosporus but the Golden Horn. Galata Bridge still provides the image of *the* bridge but is more manageable in size and includes the historic silhouette of Istanbul as a background. According to Ahmet Gürata, "despite the differences in their origin and genre, the similarities [between the foreign films that take place in Istanbul] are striking. They often use the same landmarks, starting with the Galata Bridge and ending at the Grand Bazaar via the Blue Mosque."[35]

Nevertheless, the bridge over the Bosporus is, without a doubt, the most circulated image of Istanbul. In fact, the bridge as a visual element representing Istanbul is used so often in almost everything from books to films that one wonders what was used before the first bridge was built in 1973. It seems that the bridge was used as a metaphor for Turkey's position before it was even built. Derek Williams, a British documentary director, for instance, made a short film in 1967 entitled *Turkey: The Bridge*. The film was part of a series commissioned by British Petroleum (BP) and was nominated for an Oscar that same year. According to the British Film Institute, the film is about "Turkey's place through history as a bridge between Europe

---

35 Gürata, Ahmet (2011), "City of Intrigues: Istanbul as an Exotic Attraction," *World Film Locations: Istanbul*, ed. Ozlem Koksal, London: Intellect. pp. 25.

English and Turkish, as well as the form in which the titles are written in the posters, and in the accompanying merchandise for the film, such as the music CD. The Turkish title of the film *Istanbul Hatırası/Memento of Istanbul*, is taken from a well-known, nostalgic song by Sezen Aksu, which she also performs in the film.[32] The song is performed in the singer's home, in a room overlooking the Bosporus. The large windows of the room are veiled slightly by transparent curtains, creating a blurry nostalgic image of Bosporus, as it serves as the background. As Aksu sings, Akın cuts to black-and-white photographs. These were taken by the prominent photographer Ara Güler, and are an equally well-known and nostalgic representations of the city.[33]

What is more, the title reminds the audience of the old street photographers. Now out of fashion, it involved taking pictures of people on demand in front of a curtain that was inscribed with the words "Istanbul Hatırası," with the letter "r" reversed, as in a mirror-image. The image immediately triggers nostalgic feelings, as is often the case with black-and-white photographs and old films.[34] Akın duplicates this practice in the Turkish poster by using a reversed "r."

Akın's generous use of the bridge, both as a visual element and as a metaphor, can also be read as way of creating a nostalgic idea of the city, the city as bridging cultures. However, the conception of the bridge itself is

---

32 The song mourns the past, a memory of Istanbul and perhaps a lover, mentioning old sepia photographs as well as the Markiz Patisserie, which was once a famous meeting point in the Beyoğlu district. After closing down, the patisserie kept its doors locked. The unchanged interior was visible through its windows to passers-by. In 2003 it reopened, however, unable to regain its past success, the location is now occupied by a coffee shop chain.

33 For a discussion of these photographs in relation to collective memory, see İpek Türeli in this volume.

34 The capacity of black-and-white images to trigger nostalgia, and their affiliation to the past is not self-evident but was instead constructed in the last few decades. Although I refer in particular to the lost practice of street photographers, and their image in old Turkish films, the relationship between black-and-white and the past is complicated. İpek Türeli in this volume touches upon the subject. For a detailed discussion see: Misek, Richard (2010), *Chromatic Cinema: A History of Screen Color*, London: Blackwell.

tural make-up. As Pamuk writes what he remembers of the city of his childhood, he focuses on the changes the city underwent, and contends that the best word to describe Istanbul is *hüzün*, which can be translated as melancholia. Left untranslated in the English version of the book, *hüzün* is, according to Pamuk, a "feeling that is unique to Istanbul and that binds its people together."[30]

Göktürk, in her article, mentions another book published by the Turkish Ministry of Culture and Tourism in collaboration with the Turkish Foundation of Cinema and Audiovisual Culture (TÜRSAK). According to Göktürk, the book, which was published to market Istanbul to the likes of international production companies, emphasizes "diversity in relation to the coexistence and mutual tolerance of three faiths (Judaism, Christianity and Islam)." Comparing this particular book's approach to Akın's Istanbul, Göktürk says that while the book's take on Istanbul is nostalgic, Akın's film "offers a different vision of life" promoting "a less nostalgic take on diversity by featuring Kurdish and Romani performers and putting travelling mediators on stage."[31]

Two things are worthy of mention in Göktürk's approach. The first one is the ways in which Göktürk compares the book to the film. While this specific book is intended for marketing purposes, the film is a cultural artifact about the same material. This comparison reveals the assumption that films like *Crossing the Bridge* inherently contribute to marketing the cities they represent. The second point is about producing nostalgia. Contrary to the author's statement that the film offers a counter perspective to nostalgic projects such as Orhan Pamuk's book on Istanbul, it could be argued that Akın's take on the city and its diversity is also nostalgic since he too creates a feeling of loss. What is mourned is the disappearance of the harmonious coexistence of different cultures. This is very much felt as the rhythm of the film slows down towards the end when the situation of the Kurds within the Turkish Republic, and their struggle for cultural and human rights, is mentioned in the film. The problem here is not the mourned loss, but the assumption that such harmony actually existed at some point.

There are a number of visual and narrative elements in which Akın's nostalgic approach become visible. One of these is the chosen title, both in

---

30   Pamuk (2005), *Istanbul*, p. 115.
31   Ibid, p.193

the city, juxtaposing shots of transsexuals, drunks, the middle class, the homeless, the youth of the city, in general its inhabitants, all serving to create a vibrant image of the city. But what makes all this special? Are they not scenes one can encounter almost anywhere in the world? Could this not be London, Berlin, Mexico City or indeed Lisbon? Do these scenes serve any other purpose than reproducing an image of a diverse world city? In Akın's film, while the image track produces the familiarity, the difference is produced by the sound. The familiar images include both stereotypical representations of Istanbul, such as the shot of the bridge and sunset over Bosporus, as well as images present in any global city. The difference produced by the soundtrack includes distinct musical traditions and instruments, such as Selim Sesler's clarinet and Orhan Gencebay's *saz*, as well as the fusion of western and eastern musical traditions thought to reflect Istanbul as the unique meeting point for east and west. The music used is complemented by the sound of the streets: car alarms, streets vendors, calls for a prayer, screaming seagulls, and the sound of ferries all complete the sound of Istanbul.

The question here would be "images familiar to whom" and "sounds unique to whom." I argue that the familiarity, and therefore the difference is created with the western subject in mind. It should also be noted that although the image of Istanbul as vibrant and buzzing is the opposite of that produced in *Lisbon Story* for Lisbon as serene, traditional and frozen in time, both culminate in a similar effect: both films commodify their respective cities to a degree, creating recognizable uniqueness while erasing specificity. Their approaches to these cities contribute to the existing strategies deployed to market the two cities as attractive tourist destinations offering unique experiences. However, although both films dwell on nostalgic representations, Akın's relationship to the city he is representing, his idea of what is lost and the type of nostalgia he produces are different from Wenders'.

According to Deniz Göktürk, Akın offers a "counter perspective to those nostalgic projects" about Istanbul, such as Orhan Pamuk's book.[29] Nobel Prize winner Pamuk's book, *Istanbul: Memories of a City*, is an autobiographical text offering the novelist's experiences of the city, and is dominated by a feeling of loss, particularly the loss of the city's multicul-

---

29 Göktürk (2010), "Projecting Polyphony," pp.185.

city, in agreement with Akın's vision. They often include Bosporus within the frame, at times directly as the subject of the shot, at other times Bosporus serves as the background for the shot. The sequence also includes two shots of the bridge itself. It should be noted here that there are two bridges over the Bosporus connecting the European and the Asian sides of the city. However, the film creates the illusion that there is only one bridge, which then becomes *the* bridge, emphasizing singularity, enhancing the metaphoric meaning of this overused visual element.

Once Alexandre Hacke, our guide in our journey into Istanbul's music scene, is in his hotel, he opens the window and the sound of a call for prayer fills his room. We are now three minutes into the film and almost all the clichés about Istanbul have been reproduced, albeit stylishly: Bosporus dividing Europe and Asia, the bridge connecting them, which also highlights Istanbul's geographic and historic position. This is then used to emphasize its cultural diversity. The most disseminated, and the most recognizable image of Istanbul is saved for later though: the sunset over Bosporus behind the minarets of the mosques.

Akın represents both the city as well as the music scene in the city as diverse and lively. Although the popular music scene in Turkey is excluded to a large extent, the director nevertheless creates a balanced combination of old and new approaches, mainstream and alternative sounds, known and unknown musicians. The choice of musicians, a mixture of iconic stars such as Orhan Gencebay and Sezen Aksu, along with street musicians unknown to even most of the locals, as well as his choice of a guide, Alexander Hacke, a member of the influential German industrial music band Einstürzende Neubauten, well-known in the global electronic/industrial music scene, give the audience a sense of a colorful and buzzing music scene in Istanbul. With Hacke himself sometimes participating in the live sessions, we listen to diverse musical sounds in diverse places. For example, Baba Zula's music, a band that combines the psychedelic with traditional musical instruments (i.e. *saz*, *darbuka*, spoons) is heard on a boat over the Bosporus, the iconic arabesque musician Orhan Gencebay in his office/studio, the street band Siya Siyabend on the streets of Istanbul, the Kurdish singer Aynur in a hammam, the rock-band Duman in a night club. These are just some of the locations where musicians in the film perform.

The shots of Istanbul's streets, where we get a glimpse of the night-life, are supposed to make us feel the eclectic nature of the diverse life styles in

CROSSING THE BRIDGE
ISTANBUL AS A CITY OF DIVERSE SOUNDS

How do these elements, namely producing familiar uniqueness and nostalgia play into Akın's film? How does Akın deal with the task of representing the city? As a director, Akın was discovered by world cinema enthusiasts outside of Germany after his critically acclaimed *Head-on* (2004), a film that takes place partly in Hamburg, and partly in Istanbul. He made *Crossing the Bridge* following the international success of *Head-on*. As Göktürk notes,

Fatih Akın's discovery of Istanbul occurred at a time when Istanbul was on its way to becoming the third most visited city in Europe after London and Paris (7th most visited in the world with over 7 million visitors per year) and in the wake of Istanbul's selection as a European Capital of Culture. Initiatives to promote Istanbul's candidacy took shape in July 2000, and on 13 November 2006 Istanbul was officially announced a European Capital of Culture for 2010.[27]

Crossing the Bridge opens with a member of the Siya Siyabend, a band consisting of street musicians, quoting Confucius: "If you want to understand a place you need to look at the music in that place." The director then cuts to the title of the film, written in the shape of the bridge over the Bosporus. We hear one of the band members saying that Istanbul is a bridge that is "crossed by seventy-two nations,"[28] which Akın complements by cutting to a shot of the bridge from above. During this sequence, Akın cuts back and forth between his interviewees and shots of Istanbul, mostly aerial shots, briefly introducing the musicians as well as the city.

As discussed in more detail below, aerial shots do not always serve the same purpose. Their meaning and effect on the audience can change depending on the context in which they are used. However, aerial shots often create the sense of a spatially unified city: the modern metropolis is unmanageably large and aerial shots often give us manageable views. The aerial shots Akın uses in this opening sequence give the audience a sense of the

---

27 Göktürk (2010), "Projecting Polyphony," p. 181.
28 This is a phrase used in Turkish to refer to the multicultural make up of Istanbul.

evolve from the complicated relationship between cinema and the concept of time, particularly the modern conception of time: the structured, rationalized and standardized concept of time as opposed to cinema's ability to represent time. "The rationalization of time ruptures the continuum par excellence,"[24] writes Mary Ann Doane, a discussion that is also related to Benjamin's discussion of experience and modern life. Doane adds that contingency "emerges as a form of resistance to rationalization which is saturated with ambivalence [...] Time becomes heterogeneous and unpredictable, [...] accident and chance become productive."[25] Early cinema, according to Doane "gives the spectator the opportunity of witnessing the ceaseless production of meaning *out of* contingency."[26] Hence contingency becomes a way to resist the rationalization of time that breaks the continuum of experience. Cinema, being born into modernity, and having no past before it unlike most other art forms, permits resistance to the rationalization of time but also is the product of it, hence producing the shocks. Wenders' solution to making up for this loss of continuum is to have his characters make a film-within-the-film, reproducing the aesthetics of early cinema. They mount a camera on vehicles and allow it to record randomly in an effort to capture the unstructured, unexpected meaning that the city harbors. Paradoxically, Wenders is only able to do this with the technologies available to him at the time, in this case, small cameras. What is more, his aesthetic references to early cinema in the film-within-the-film, as well as the direct references to perhaps the most famous city film, i.e. *A Man With a Movie Camera* (Dziga Vertov, 1929), maintain the audience's relation to the past, to the nostalgic image on screen. The overall effect is an image of the city on screen that is unaffected by change, and yet is also a city that offers opportunities for chance encounters unique to cities, and unavailable elsewhere. This is a modern city, where anxieties turn into productive surprises through the use of the cinematic medium, a city where vastness is reduced to the manageable and unchanging neighborhood of Alfama using the grammar of nostalgia.

---

24   Doane, Marry Ann (2002), *The Emergence of Cinematic Time: Modernity, Contingency, The Archive*, Massachusetts: Harvard University Press, p. 9.
25   Ibid, p.11.
26   Ibid, p. 181.

The City in Black-and-White
Photographic Memories*

İPEK TÜRELİ

Writings on "media memories," or memories recorded by and recollected through media technologies, have touched upon the deliberate and relative uses of black-and-white visuals, especially in the cinema.[1] Yet, there seems to be relatively little reflection in terms of the media memories of cities.[2] This essay is concerned with the recycling and circulation of old, mono-

---

1   There is a growing scholarly conversation on the role of media representations on memory; e.g. Huyssen, Andreas (1995), *Twilight Memories: Marking Time in a Culture of Amnesia*, New York: Routledge; Sobchack, Vivian C. (Ed.) (1996), *The Persistence of History: Cinema, Television, and the Modern Event*, New York: Routledge; Grainge, Paul (2002), *Monochrome Memories: Nostalgia and Style in Retro America*, Westport, Conn.: Praeger; van Dijck, Jose (2007), *Mediated Memories in the Digital Age: Cultural Memory in the Present*, Stanford: Stanford University Press; Misek, Richard (2010), *Chromatic Cinema: A History of Screen Color*, Chichester, U.K. and Malden, MA: Wiley-Blackwell.
2   There is a significant body of work on the media images of cities, especially on "cinematic cities;" e.g. Alsayyad, Nezar (2006), *Cinematic Urbanism*, New York and London: Routledge; Mennel, Barabara C. (2008), *Cities and Cinema*, Milton Park, Abingdon, Oxon and New York: Routledge; Shiel, Mark and Tony Fitzmaurice (2001), *Cinema and the City: Film and Urban Societies in a Global Context*, Oxford and Malden, Mass.: Blackwell; Clarke, David B. (1997), *Cinematic City*, London and New York: Routledge.

Photograph: Derya Özkan

chromatic or black-and-white images of the city.[3] Black-and-white photography of "Old Istanbul" is viewed today by all generations in Turkey with tender regard because it shows how much the now booming city has moved away from its poorer and relatively provincial past.[4] Above all, however, it is Armenian-Turkish photographer Ara Güler's (born 1928) work from the 1950s and 1960s that stands out, and is best known among enthusiasts of the city in Istanbul, Turkey, and abroad. I argue that the photographs' black-and-whiteness contributes to their popular recirculation and reception. This representational mode helps situate photographs far away in time and turns them into an album of the past that can be recalled to imagine the future of the city as a diverse and colorful place. Professional curators, commentators, and ordinary citizens posting on Facebook alike commonly state that Güler's black-and-white pictures show how colorful the city was once upon a time. They refer to the quality and texture of social life, of course, and not to the physical sense of the term. Color here is a metaphor for social life, and paradoxically black-and-white ends up signifying color (diversity). Since the 1990s, the re-circulation of Güler's photographs has become part and parcel of the new life of black-and-white as a "nostalgia

---

3   The discussion of color (or the lack thereof) continues to attract scholarly attention. In addition to Misek (2010), *Chromatic Cinema*, and Grainge (2002), *Monochrome Memories*, see, for instance, the special issue on color in *Journal of Chinese Cinemas* 6 (3), 2012, edited by Margaret Hillenbrand. Saskia Sassen (2002) takes up black-and-white as a representational mode in her essay on Sebastiao Salgado in "Black and White Photography as Theorizing: Seeing What the Eye Cannot See," *Sociological Forum* 26 (2), pp. 438-443.

4   In a similar vein, black-and-white Turkish films from the 1950s and 1960s, mostly shot in Istanbul, are recycled in various formats. Türeli, İpek (2012), "Istanbul in Black and White: Cinematic Memory," online component to *Ars Orientalis*, Freer and Sackler Galleries, (http://www.asia.si.edu/research/articles/Istanbul-in-black-and-white.asp, accessed 18 June 2014). Türeli, İpek (2010), "Istanbul through Migrants' Eyes," in *Orienting Istanbul: Cultural Capital of Europe?*, ed. Deniz Göktürk, Levent Soysal, İpek Türeli, London: Routledge, pp. 144-64.

mode"; the lack of color signifies a distant period in the past rather than a specific time.⁵

Originally produced for journalism as photographs printed in local newspapers and illustrated magazines, often accompanying news reports, Güler's Istanbul photographs made a comeback first in the local scene, and then internationally, as art prints in exhibitions on the city held in Istanbul and abroad since the 1990s.⁶ Known among his followers as "the eye of Istanbul," or "the last poet of Istanbul," Güler is perhaps the most widely known and beloved photographer of the city.⁷ Güler's black-and-white photographs of Istanbul from the 1950s and 1960s have become synonymous with nostalgia for Istanbul's past. Nostalgia, here, denotes a collective feeling, "a longing for a home that no longer exists or has never existed."⁸ This yearning arises from dissatisfaction with the present. Just as for a place, it can also be a yearning for a different time.

Local critics have been praising Güler as an artist—a label he has never fully accepted, preferring to call himself a "witness" or a "visual historian," arguing that photography is not autonomous like art (in the modernist sense).⁹ Despite these assertions, newspaper and television reports claimed that Güler was not pleased when an exhibitions of his Istanbul work, "Istanbul'da Alınteri" (Sweat of the Laborer in Istanbul), was mounted in the Taksim subway station in the spring of 2008. Reportedly, Güler had supplied the photographs but was not informed about how they would be exhibited. He was quoted as saying that the photographs in the show, organized jointly by the Chamber of Trade and the Istanbul Municipality, needed to be exhibited in an art gallery, and that ordinary metro passengers

---

5 Misek (2010), *Chromatic Cinema*, p. 116. Also, Jameson, Frederic (1984), "Postmodernism, or the Cultural Logic of Late Capitalism," *New Left Review* 146, pp. 53-92.
6 Türeli, İpek (2010), "Ara Güler's Photography of 'Old Istanbul' and Cosmopolitan Nostalgia," *History of Photography* 34 (3), pp. 300-313.
7 Güler, Ara and Enis Batur (2003), *Istanbul'un Son Şairi Ara Güler*, Istanbul: Yapı Kredi. I make the suggestion that the photographer is "loved" based on the circulation of his news in media and social media (e.g. fan pages).
8 Boym, Svetlana (2001), *The Future of Nostalgia*, New York: Basic, p. xiii.
9 Tavlaş, Nezih (2009), *Foto Muhabiri: Ara Güler'in Hayat Hikâyesi*, Istanbul: Fotoğrafevi.

who walked by his photographs in the station would not understand them.[10] The irony, of course, is that most of these photographs had originally been taken for newspapers and illustrated magazines, not for exhibition in galleries.

Güler's career as a professional photographer took off in the context of an expanding print media, and in relation to the dramatic physical and social transformations in the city of the 1950s, a decade marked by urban renewal and rapid population growth with internal migration. However, the recent reframing of Güler's work through a selection of his earlier photographs documenting the changes on the streets of Istanbul has a much different purpose. The photographer has by no means been a passive observer in this process. This reframing intends to promote a popularized longing for the multi-ethnic, multi-religious past of the city, the loss of which the photographer also laments, as he explicitly states in interviews.[11] Güler's pictures are powerful today because they embalm the city in a way that is particularly useful to nostalgic accounts of the city's cosmopolitan past. The work is significant not only because of the photographs' content but also due to its re-circulation in a variety of media, ranging from books and exhibitions to the built environment.

The revival of Güler's work made his name synonymous with urban nostalgia that was amplified by the realm of popular consumption of visual cultural products in the early 1990s.[12] It corresponded with the beginnings of an official government effort to transform Istanbul into a "capital of culture"—reflective of the global turn from managerial to entrepreneurial city governance and the concomitant efforts to use "culture" to market cities.[13] More precisely, it is possible to date Güler's revival to 1992, when

---

10 "Ara Güler'den, Belediye'ye Sergi Tepkisi," CNNTürk, 6 March 2008 (http://www.cnnturk.com/2008/kultur-sanat/diger/03/06/ara.gulerden.belediyeye.sergi.tepkisi/435105.0/index.html, accessed 18 June 2014).

11 Kinzer, Stephen, "Turkey's Passionate Interpreter to the World," *New York Times*, 13 April 1997.

12 Boym (2011), *The Future of Nostalgia*, p. xiii.

13 The literature on this topic is vast. For an earlier and succinct account of this transformation, see this classic article: Harvey, David (1989), "From Managerialism to Entrepreneurialism: The Transformation in Urban Governance in

Turkey's Ministry of Culture and Tourism declared 1993 to be the "Year of Istanbul," and recruited the History Foundation to manage and organize the celebrations. One of the self-designated missions of this foundation, a then newly established non-governmental organization composed of prominent Turkish social scientists and historians, was to challenge official historical narratives by focusing on the everyday social and cultural history of Istanbul from a minor history perspective.[14] As part of the celebrations, it organized Güler's first Istanbul exhibition, "Istanbul, an Endless Reportage," his twenty-second solo show.[15] A coffee-table catalogue, *A Photographical Sketch on Lost Istanbul*, subsequently presented Güler's selected Istanbul work in print in 1994.[16] Many other photographic exhibitions and books followed in this vein, all with the intention of reproducing the lost Istanbul Güler had captured.

The irony in the valorization of photography as an art of the original, the photographers as artists in the modernist sense, and the move of documentary, news, and even scientific photography (e.g. topographic views) into galleries and museums in the 1980s was problematized early on by art critics such as Christopher Phillips, Rosalind Krauss, and Abigail Solomon-Godeau.[17] Douglas Crimp observes that photographs which may have pre-

---

Late Capitalism," *Geografiska Annaler. Series B, Human Geography* 71 (1), The Roots of Geographical Change: 1973 to the Present, pp. 3-17.

14   See the website of the organization for a list of founders and activities: www.tarihvakfi.org.tr/ (accessed 18 June 2014).

15   This information is based on the list of exhibitions provided in Ara Güler's book of photographs (Güler, Ara [1994], *A Photographical Sketch on Lost Istanbul, Istanbul*: Dünya Yayınları). The list covers exhibitions until 2008, in the seventh printing (2008) of the book that I own.

16   Ibid. Güler's book was published simultaneously in English, and Turkish, the latter with the title, *Eski Istanbul Anıları* (Memories of Old Istanbul).

17   Phillips, Christopher (1982), "The Judgment Seat of Photography," *October* 22, pp. 27-63. Kraus, Rosalind (1982), "Photography's Discursive Spaces: Landscape/View," *Art Journal* 42 (4), The Crisis in the Discipline, pp. 311-319. Solomon-Godeau, Abigail (1991), "Canon Fodder: Authoring Eugène Atget," in *Photography at the Dock: Essays on Photographic History, Institutions, and Practices*, ed. Abigail Solomon-Godeau, Minneapolis: University of Minnesota Press, pp. 28-51.

viously been illustrations in books, and organized in the space of the library by topic, came to be classified by the "artists" who made them, leading to, for instance, photography that was formerly characterized as "urban poverty" to recirculate as shows by Jacob Riis (1849-1914) or Lewis Hine (1874-1940).[18] Echoing such developments, Güler's photographs of the poor urban working classes taken in the 1950s and 1960s were recalled from the archive, detached from their original presentations in the media, typically as accompaniments to texts, and moved into exhibition contexts. The recirculation (and popularity) of these photographs since the 1990s meant a small section of his work came to be characterized as his artistic signature. However, his work has a larger scope and range, both in terms of topic and technique. The photographs featured in a recent Smithsonian exhibit, for instance, are high-definition gelatin-silver prints of historic monuments in rural landscapes such as that of an (unpeopled) Ishak Paşa Palace in Doğubayazıt in Eastern Turkey.[19]

What kinds of meanings are attributed to the images of the urban poor of Istanbul when they are taken from their original contexts and then recirculated in the present? In a previous article, I focused on a detailed comparative reading of the circulation of different sets of photographs from this earlier phase of the photographer's work.[20] I argued that those that do not touch on politically sensitive topics, such as the dispossession of non-Muslims, and those that instead reflect on urban poverty, rural-to-urban migration and the challenges of rapid urbanization, are more likely to recirculate. Contemporary re-circulation is also revealing in that it shows the centrality and utility of the photographs to advance cosmopolitan nostalgia.[21]

A typical example is Güler's photograph of two boatmen, dated 1956, and which adorns the cover of his 1994 *Lost Istanbul*.[22]

---

18   Crimp, Douglas (1993), *On the Museum's Ruins*, Cambridge, MA: MIT, p. 74.
19   "Ara Güler's Anatolia," exhibition in Arthur M. Sackler Gallery, Smithsonian Museum of Asian Art: Washington DC, United States, 14 December 2013—21 July 2014.
20   Türeli (2010), "Ara Güler's Photography," pp. 300-313.
21   Ibid.
22   Güler (1994), *Lost Istanbul*.

Boatmen in the Golden Horn, Old Galata Bridge and the New Mosque. Ara Güler, Turkey, 1956 (Ara Güler/Magnum Photos).

This photograph also features on the cover of another author's book that tries to recover the memories of a multi-religious, multi-cultural city.[23] Neither the book's title, "Yesterday's Istanbul: The Dissolution of a Multi-religious, Multi-linguistic Mosaic," nor its content are about these boatmen. The photograph does not communicate in itself anything specific about the two people, their religion or language. The viewer can hardly make out the figures' physical features; they are backlit, and discernable only as silhouettes. The figures' postures and attire only suggest their socio-economic status: working class and poor. Their loose jackets and flat caps (as opposed to rimmed hats) situate them in a loose temporality.[24] The figures can

---

23 Eksen, İlhan (2002), *Dünkü Istanbul: Çok Dinli, Çok Dilli Mozaiğin Dağılışı*, Istanbul: Sel Yayıncılık.
24 Between 1925, when the Republic's "hat revolution" encouraged men to give up their fez and other traditional hats, and 1950, men were rarely seen out and about without a hat.

be identified as boatmen because of their positioning in front of the two small boats, the silhouettes of which merge with the boatmen's. This dark foreground is set against a grey middle ground consisting of the Golden Horn and the Old Galata Bridge crossing it, and a background of Yeni Camii, hovering right above the figures with its domes and minarets yet veiled by a heavy fog. This is a city where small boats still operate, a city where electric streetlights may not have yet arrived. Consumed today, the photograph is nostalgic of a bygone era, but it is not precise in its message. Whatever or whichever time one is nostalgic about, the photograph allows the viewer to project on it. The appeal of Güler's photographs is not necessarily derived from their relation to an original subject or from the texts that may or may not accompany them, but from their potential to evoke human compassion without commitment for change. Güler's recycled photographs do not lend themselves to a programmatic reading. They do not contrast the old and the new, in favor of the new; nor do they show their subjects in passive poses that invite the intervention of the viewers.

PHOTOGRAPHS IN THE EXHIBITION

Güler's well-known Istanbul photographs have been reproduced in many forms, and their inclusion in exhibitions, magazines and books has provided varied opportunities for imagining "Old Istanbul." Some commercial ventures have gone even further, advertising physical environments in which customers may immerse themselves in Güler's work. Two striking examples are the Ara Café, located in a building owned by Güler in the district of Beyoğlu (a building that also houses his studio), and Point Hotel, a boutique hotel in the district of Talimhane where Güler was born. These two commercial spaces have been likened to "museums" in promotional reports.[25]

---

25 MacEacheran, Mike, "Istanbul's New Museum Manifesto," *BBC Travel*, last modified 20 December 2012 (http://www.bbc.com/travel/feature/20121217-Istanbuls-new-museum-manifesto, accessed 18 June 2014).

It was Güler who chose the black-and-white photographs from the 1950s and 1960s to be placed in these spaces.[26] Photographers visiting Istanbul on the occasion of the Magnum exhibition, "Turkey by Magnum," at the Istanbul Modern Museum were hosted at the sponsoring Point Hotel, and allegedly, they too marveled at the museum-like feeling of the hotel's decor where rooms, restaurant, lobby and other common spaces are adorned with Güler's works.[27] Güler further helped promote the hotel, e.g. by posing in front of his photographs on the walls.[28]

At the nearby Ara Café, customers eat on paper placemats on which Güler's well-known Istanbul photographs are printed, while they study large-format reproductions of his images on the walls. This gives the café customers the possibility to imagine that at any minute the photographer himself may come down from his studio to join them. Indeed he is often spotted there, and he has given many of his interviews in this space.[29]

The exhibitionary aspect of these two spaces may be linked to the growth of new private museums and alternative exhibition spaces in the city during the past two decades. Looking beyond Istanbul, however, it is difficult not to notice that the use of black-and-white or monochrome prints in cafes, bars and similar commercial collective spaces emerged also in the 1990s as a "signature of designer chic" in metropolitan centers.[30] The doubling of these two commercial spaces, Ara Café and Point Hotel, as exhibition spaces is indicative of how the reframing of Güler's images is part of a broader, transnational cultural and commercial production.

As with most constructions of memory, this process of evoking "Old Istanbul" entails remembering and forgetting in a dialectical relationship,

---

26 Özarslan, Sevinç, "Talimhane'de Bir Ara Otel," *Zaman*, 14 October 2006 (http://www.zaman.com.tr/newsDetail_openPrintPage.action?newsId=793265, accessed 18 June 2014).

27 "Turkey by Magnum" was held at the Istanbul Museum of Modern Art 17 February—20 May 2007. The Point Hotel was the "exhibition accommodation supporter." (http://www.Istanbulmodern.org/en/exhibitions/past-exhibitions/turkey-by-magnum_166.html, accessed 18 June 2014)

28 Özarslan (2006), "Talimhane'de Bir Ara Otel."

29 E.g. Adıgüzel, Hacer (2003), "Ara Güler ile Sanat, Fotograf ve Istanbul'a Dair," *Istanbul* 8: pp. 36-39.

30 Grainge (2002), *Monochrome Memories*, p. xiv.

where memory and history are entangled rather than oppositional, as Pierre Nora argued in his famous work on *lieux de mémoire*.[31] The relationship between photography and memory is also complex. Photography is popularly conceived of as an act of remembrance, despite the fact that some of photography's best-known critics, such as Siegfried Kracauer and Roland Barthes, argue that photography and memory "are at odds," and that photography "blocks memory."[32] In contrast, the historian of photography Geoffrey Batchen has suggested that photographs are not necessarily produced to bring the past to the present but to situate the self in relation to an unknown future.[33] In the context of Istanbul, the recalling of old photographs from the archive serves a similar purpose. In a city under the strain of economic neoliberalization, an older or other time and place can be treated as a *belle époque*, a time when citizens were imagined to be more civilized and tolerant toward each other. This is a vaguely defined temporality, early to mid-twentieth-century, as signified in the photograph of the two boatmen. Güler's photographs have thus been instrumental in imagining a more harmonious past as the basis for an "open city" of the future.[34]

---

31 Nora, Pierre (1989), "Between Memory and History: *Les Lieux de Mémoire*," *Representations* 26, Special Issue: Memory and Counter-Memory, pp. 7-24.

32 The first quote is from Kracauer, Siegfried (1995), "Photography," in *The Mass Ornament: Weimar Essays*, Cambridge, Mass.: Harvard University Press, p. 50, cited in Batchen, Geoffrey (2004), *Forget Me Not: Photography and Remembrance*, New York: Princeton Architectural Press, p. 16. The second is from Barthes, Roland (1982), *Camera Lucida: Reflections on Photography*, London: Vintage, p. 91, cited in Batchen, *Forget Me Not* (2004), p. 15.

33 Batchen (2004), *Forget Me Not*, p. 98.

34 In contemporary urban planning literature, the term "open city" is sometimes invoked to describe a lack of growth controls that might otherwise be used to divert unwanted migrants. As such, "open city" represents an ideal at the opposite end of a spectrum from what Richard Sennett has called the "brittle city"—a closed, over-determined system that denies chance encounters, narrative possibilities, and growth over time. Sennett, Richard (2008), "The Open City," in *The Endless City*, ed. Ricky Burdett and Dejan Sudjic, London: Phaidon. See also: Rieniets, Tim, Sigler, Jennifer and Kees Christiaanse (Ed.s) (2009), *Open City: Designing Coexistence*, Catalogue of the 4th Architecture

Photography is one of several mediums through which "Old Istanbul" is curated. Areas of Istanbul are being transformed into images of idealized pasts, as can be seen in the manufactured streetscape of what used to be known as Algeria (Cezayir) Street, now "French Street," a themed touristic environment.[35] Amy Mills' work on Kuzguncuk, a Bosphorus village in Istanbul, reveals that the nostalgic rendering of the district as a traditional cosmopolitan Istanbul neighbourhood in both media and individual narratives is highly selective, obscures past tensions, and even wipes out the actual histories of non-Muslim displacement.[36]

This process of curating the past for the present is not exclusive to Istanbul. Many cities are undergoing similar processes. For instance, in the context of Eastern Europe, Svetlana Boym has observed that "the urban renewal taking place in the present is no longer futuristic but nostalgic; the city imagines its future by improvising on its past."[37] But among other media, photography has proved particularly instrumental because of its indexicality, or truth claim due to the physical relationship between the object photographed and the photograph. In relation to Damascus, anthropologist Christa Salamandra discusses the revalorization of the "Old Damascus" among the Damascene elite in the 1990s. She explains, "Photographs are among the most important means of reconstructing a lost place of the past."[38] Many exhibits about Old Damascus were sponsored by The Society of Friends of Damascus, established in 1977 and characterized as an elite group established for socialization more than activism aimed at preservation. Here, appreciation of Old Damascus provided a loose group

---

Biennale in Rotterdam, held from 24 September 2009 to 10 January 2010, Amsterdam: SUN Architecture.

35   Prehl, Susanne (2008), "Whose Space, Whose Culture? Struggle for Cultural Representation in 'French Street' of Istanbul," in *Public Istanbul: Spaces and Spheres of the Urban*, ed. Frank Eckardt and Kathrin Wildner, Bielefeld: Transcript, pp. 299-318.

36   Mills, Amy (2010), *Streets of Memory: Landscape, Tolerance, and National Identity in Istanbul*, Athens, Ga.: University of Georgia Press.

37   Boym (2001), *The Future of Nostalgia*, p. 75.

38   Salamandra, Christa (2004), *A New Old Damascus: Authenticity and Distinction in Urban Syria*, Bloomington: Indiana University Press, p. 79.

boundary or "distinction" à la Bourdieu despite the fact that the group's members did not live there.

In relation to Harbin in China, anthropologist Yukiko Koga explains that the colonial era under Russia is nostalgically embraced to differentiate Harbin as a tourist destination.[39] Destroyed during the Cultural Revolution, the Russian-built St. Sophia Cathedral was restored in the mid-1990s as part of a Beijing-originating national effort to protect historic sites. It then became the "face of the city." Inside the building, a popular photographic exhibition of "Old Harbin" celebrates "Western" buildings from the early twentieth century, although it provides limited information on the buildings and edits out the Russian invasion. This contrasts sharply with some of the nearby museums that seek to educate the public about past atrocities and imperialism. Koga observes, "Nostalgia for Old Harbin is a displaced form of social criticism of contemporary Harbin."[40] Comparably, the appreciation of "Old Istanbul" emerged as a means of group distinction, as well as displaced social criticism. It tied in well with official agendas of city marketing.

What do individuals find in Güler's photographs? In his introduction to *Ara Güler's Istanbul* (published by Thames and Hudson, 2009), novelist Orhan Pamuk explains, "The Istanbul of the 1950s and 1960s [...] is nowhere as well documented, preserved and protected as it is in the photographs of Ara Güler," echoing a popular sentiment that dominates the reception of the work.[41] Despite the resistant nostalgia (here, the resistance is to change), which the photographer's fans may project onto individual photographs, there is an official desire to incorporate the body of work into economic and political projects. Güler has become the quasi-official photographer for city administration and publicity efforts toward city and country branding in Europe. In fact, the Thames and Hudson volume was the English edition of a French-language publication that followed an exhibi-

---

39 Koga, Yukiko (2008), "'The Atmosphere of a Foreign Country': Harbin's Architectural Inheritance," in *The Entrepreneurial City: Image, Memory, Spectacle*, ed. Anne M. Cronin and Kevin Hetherington Consuming, New York: Routledge, pp. 221-53, p. 229.

40 Ibid, p. 232.

41 Pamuk, Orhan (2009), "Foreword," *Ara Güler's Istanbul: 40 Years of Photographs*, Thames & Hudson: London.

tion of the photographer's work in 2009. It was part of the Turkish Cultural Season in France. This nine-month "season," intended to introduce Turkey's culture to France, was planned during the presidency of Jacques Chirac but was ironically realized during that of Nicolas Sarkozy, who was known for his anti-Turkey rhetoric vocalizing anxiety over Turkey's increasing presence and influence in Europe.[42]

One of the most recent occasions in which the government turned to Güler was immediately following the Gezi protests. The Beyoğlu (District) Municipality advertised in July 2013 that Güler shot the "Photograph of (A Mind at) Peace," of a Ramadan *iftar* (fast-breaking) dinner on the very site of the protests on Taksim Square.[43] Public Ramadan feasts had been set up on the Square in previous years as well, but this time the sit-down dinner with guests including representatives of religious minorities was staged in official defiance of the Gezi protests.[44] The photograph attributed to Güler and released to the media was in color, taken from a raised central stage and showing the many dinner tables on Taksim square radiating out. The image was a somewhat ordinary photograph resembling a wedding photograph, and overtly promotional. It was circulated by the government in government-leaning mainstream news media. This was in part a response to the documentation of the protests by a new generation of activist photographers, such as those of the collective Nar Photos documenting the protests and showing government and security forces' violence perpetrated on civilians, and circulating in social media.[45]

---

42 See http://www.digitalbridges.eu/?p=21 (accessed 18 June 2014).

43 "Taksim'in 'huzur fotoğrafını' Ara Güler çekti," *Staryaşam*, 31 July 2013 (http://haber.stargazete.com/yasam/taksimin-huzur-fotografini-ara-guler-cekti/haber-777650, accessed 18 June 2014).

44 This time, municipally organized Ramadan fast-breaking dinners were challenged by those organized by the group "Anti-capitalist Muslims" in the form of *yeryüzü sofraları*, or earth dinners, spread on the ground and attended by Gezi supporters from all walks of life.

45 Devrim Gürsel, Zeynep, Interview with Nar Photos Collective, "Covering Gezi: Reflecting on Photographing Daily Life during Extraordinary Events," *Jadaliyya*, 24 June 2013 (http://photography.jadaliyya.com/pages/index/12390/covering-gezi_reflecting-on-photographing-daily-li, accessed 23 October 2014).

In this case, it was not the black-and-white photographs from the 1950s and 1960s that were shown in government-initiated marketing-oriented "Old Istanbul" exhibitions, but the photographer's very persona that was claimed and incorporated by conservative politicians and their media apparatus. As a citizen of Turkey of Armenian ethnicity, the photographer was called in to stand in as evidence of the tolerance of the current government under *Justice and Development Party* (Adalet ve Kalkınma Partisi or AKP). In fact, the AKP has frequently featured non-Muslims in its promotional efforts to present Istanbul as a cosmopolitan city.[46] The photographer's fans were in shock that Güler would take such a photograph, and this led to discussions in social media and write-ups in mainstream print media, both underscoring how Güler's work is received and read as a form of resistance.[47]

THE AESTHETICS OF BLACK-AND-WHITE

Black-and-whiteness as a representational mode is an important aspect of Güler's work and its reception. Black-and-white photography is mostly theorized in the realm of film studies. Black-and-white footage is often

---

46 E.g. *I'm Istanbul/Ben Istanbulum* (2007), Istanbul: Istanbul Büyük Şehir Belediyesi Kültür A.Ş. In this book, supposedly representative Istanbulites provide short write-ups about the multiculturalism in the city based on personalized narratives. Aret Vartanyan says in the first piece: "I am proud to say, 'I am from Istanbul. My family has lived here for centuries,' when I was asked about my home country [...] It was inevitable to have colorful and unforgettable childhood memories as my father is Armenian, my mother is Greek, my grandmother is Jewish, my grandfather is Russian, and my cousins are Muslim." All but one of the selected contributors to this publication bear non-Muslim minority names, a misleading overrepresentation of members of the now dwindling non-Muslim minority population.

47 Eğrikavuk, Işıl, "Taksim'in Huzuru Resmini Kim Çekti?" *Radikal*, 5 August 2013 (http://www.radikal.com.tr/yazarlar/isil_egrikavuk/taksimin_huzuru_resmini_kim_cekti-1144905, accessed 18 June 2014). See the comments of disappointment under a Facebook posting by another famous local photographer: https://www.facebook.com/muratgermen65/posts/10152068145359409 (accessed 18 June 2014).

associated with alternative reality: dreams, fantasies, memories, or the historical past. In art films, directors may also use black-and-white or desaturated imagery to create a sense of "truthfulness," rather than "reality" (as in the work of the Turkish director Nuri Bilge Ceylan or the Russian director Andrei Tarkovski).[48] Art critic Anne Hollander suggests:

[...] early combinations of printed words and pictures helped the association between black-and-white printed representations and unadorned truthfulness that gives the term "graphic" one of its meanings. We have built on this association the idea that if a picture is in black and white, it can be apprehended more clearly, even though it may be enjoyed less. By extension photographs and movies in black and white are considered good because they are so true, not because they are so real. Their often brilliant beauty rests on this. "Living color" may be more lifelike and more delicious, but, like life itself, it is also more distracting, entrancing and misleading.[49]

Black-and-white imagery alludes to the veracity of inner worlds—in contrast to a more accurate, and perhaps more enjoyable, chromatic reproduction of the external world. The association of black-and-white with truth is also based on a deep suspicion of the medium's heightened indexicality with high definition color photography.

The common association of black-and-white with "pastness" is a post-1960s phenomenon. It reverses, in fact, the relationship initiated in Hollywood's classical period with the use of color imagery to connote fantasy-as-inner world.[50] Most memorable may be the association of color with fantasy in the *The Wizard of Oz* (1939), where Dorothy's real black-and-white life in Kansas contrasts sharply with the colored world of Oz. Had it been shot today, real life in Kansas would most likely have been shot in high definition colour with Oz in monochrome.

Although color photography was invented in the 1860s, and color was used in film as early as the 1920s, black-and-white photography remained

---

48   Johnson, Vida T. and Graham Petrie (1994), *The Films of Andrei Tarkovsky*, Bloomington: Indiana University Press, pp. 188-89.
49   Hollander, Anne (1989), *Moving Pictures*, New York: Alfred A. Knopf, p. 33.
50   Misek, Richard (2010), *Chromatic Cinema: A History of Screen Color*, Chichester, West Sussex, U.K.: Wiley-Blackwell.

the norm for motion pictures (including newsreels and cinema, etc.) until the 1950s (the 1970s in Turkey). This is what produced the early association of black-and-white with reality. However, now that high-definition color media saturate everyday life so completely, black-and-white imagery has shifted to connote something closer to "truth" (and the inner world) as opposed to "reality."

Paul Grainge's discussion of "monochrome memories" is particularly useful in thinking through the aesthetics of black-and-white in the 1990s, and when and why black-and-white is preferred over color. He suggests black-and-whiteness emerged as a "visual discourse" in the 1990s.[51] The use and experience of monochrome surged across a range of mediums and forms—not only news photography but also corporate advertising and commodified designer chic.[52] Through a close reading of the editorial choices in *Time* magazine to use black-and-white or color in its cover designs, Grainge makes the argument that monochrome or black-and-white transform news into chronicle. In the era of online news and instant communication, the news magazine has had to reinvent itself as provider of in-depth stories rather than news: black-and-white was used to "chronicle" while color was used for breaking news.[53] A related argument, echoing Susan Sontag's work on photography and Frederic Jameson's on film, is the valorization of blac-and-white as a nostalgia mode. In the context of Istanbul, Güler's work has to be understood not only in terms of representational content, but also through its circulation among a broad range of nostalgia modes for "Old Istanbul." The revival of Güler's work and its popular reception is connected to transnational developments in the image regime.

GÜLER'S CONVERSATIONS WITH STREET PHOTOGRAPHERS

It may sound peculiar to anyone familiar with the history of the technology of the photographic medium that black-and-white is associated here with the 1950s and 1960s, despite the fact that by that time, color had become

---

51 Grainge (2002), *Monochrome Memories*.
52 Ibid, xiii-xiv.
53 Ibid, pp. 67-97.

the standard in photography, cinema, and TV broadcasting in North America and Europe. Contextualizing Güler's work transnationally is necessary here. His approach to photography is part of the genre "street photography" in vogue from 1930s to the 1960s, and which developed in connection to the small format camera.[54] Like earlier social documenters, street photographers remained suspicious of color and adhered to black-and-white.[55] Güler's photographs foreground individuals, men and women going about with their usual business or activity, while acknowledging the photographer's presence. Children pose for him with excitement. The background is the old city, the dilapidated wooden houses, and crooked streets. The reception of his photographs, however, needs to be considered in relation to other albums of urban nostalgia, such as "Old Paris," as invoked by Sontag.

A distinction between documentary and street photography may be useful here. Documentary photographers approach their topics with the intention to document or chronicle a social type, e.g. the poor or oppressed, or a historical condition (e.g. The Great Depression in the US, 1929) and with the intention to incite certain responses in their more privileged viewers in order to encourage change. Jacob Riis (1849-1914) chose as his subject matter crowded and unsanitary interiors, alleys and courts; Lewis Hine photographed laborers and recently arrived immigrants; Weegee (Arthur Felling, 1899-1968) photographed the extremes of the urban crowd (e.g. murder victims, muggers). Street photographers also concern themselves with everyday life but lack the reformist tone; they instead seek to invoke self-reflection.[56]

In his work, Güler celebrates street life with compassion, yet his photographs lack the reformist zeal. In his position as the photographer of his city, Güler can be compared with Eugène Atget (1857-1927). Self-admittedly much influenced by "the pictures on the run" (*images à la sauvatte*) of Henri Cartier-Bresson (1908-2004), one of the co-founders of the famous Magnum photo agency in Paris in 1947, Güler experimented

---

54   Clarke, Graham (1997), *The City in Photography*, Oxford; New York: Oxford University Press.
55   Scot, Clive (2007), "The Street-Photographic and the Documentary," *in Street Photography: From Atget to Cartier-Bresson*, ed. Clive Scot, London and New York: I.B. Tauris, pp. 57-89.
56   Ibid.

with many different approaches to street photography over the years.[57] Güler's photographs reveal conversations with the works of prominent photographers of his day, as well as his awareness of seminal precedents.

In order to explain why Güler's work aligns with street photography, Riis' "Street Arabs at Night" (1890) can be contrasted with Güler's "Wooden houses and children in the Gypsy quarter, Şişhane" (1969) as both feature children as central characters.[58]

Street Arabs at Night. Jacob Riis, USA, 1890 (The Jacob A. Riis Collection, Museum of the City of New York).

---

57   Cartier-Bresson, Henri (1952), *The Decisive Moment*, New York: Simon and Schuster. Also see: Tavlaş, Nezih (2009), *Foto Muhabiri Ara Güler*, Istanbul: Fotoğrafevi Yayınları, pp. 112-116.

58   The Riis photograph illustrates the seventeenth chapter with the same title of the Riis' (1890) *How the Other Half Lives: Studies among the Tenements of New York*, with illustrations chiefly from photographs taken by the author, New York: Charles Scribner's Sons.

Wooden Houses and Children in the Gypsy Quarter, Şişhane. Ara Güler, Turkey, 1969 (Ara Güler/Magnum Photos).

In Riis' famous shot, the bundling of the children at the rear accentuates their need for space. They are passive (sleeping), and not engaging the photographer or using space—such composition and framing invite the viewer into the space of the photograph to act. In contrast, Güler's photograph depicts a decaying inner-city neighborhood.[59] Children inhabit the foreground of the picture. Poverty does not seem to weigh on the children or the few women in this environment. One of the boys almost throws himself at the photographer; with his eyes fixed on the camera, he is ready to become its subject. The viewer is thus invited to take an interest in the subjects, but not necessarily to get to know them or to take action. The photograph, by itself, does not even try to persuade its audience to conclude

---

59   Güler's photograph is the first photograph of a 10-day photo essay, entitled "Al İşte Istanbul," and originally co-produced with author Çetin Altan for the local daily *Akşam*. For a more detailed discussion, see Türeli (2010), "Ara Güler's Photography."

that such conditions should change. All it does is evoke a generalized compassion. While his compositions and subject matters are varied, in general, Güler's human subjects have agency; they do not call upon the viewer to act on their behalf.

One of Güler's famous photographs, from 1956, entitled "Winter arrives in the Sirkeci district of Istanbul," is reminiscent of Alfred Stieglitz's (1864-1946) famous photograph "The Terminal" (1893) because of the subject matter: the horse-drawn carriage on a snowy, difficult day in the city.

Winter Arrives in the Sirkeci District of Istanbul. Ara Güler, Turkey, 1956 (Ara Güler/Magnum Photos).

In the Stieglitz shot, a Harlem streetcar is waiting for passengers in front of the Post Office while the driver is watering the horses.[60] In the Güler shot, a basic horse-drawn cart, with a single horse to transport goods is moving on

---

60 View the photograph on Getty Images: http://www.getty.edu/art/gettyguide/artObjectDetails?artobj=69262 (accessed 18 June 2014).

the tram-track while pulled by the driver; this is a portrait-oriented photograph; the sides are framed by apartment buildings on both sides of the already narrow street, accentuating the tightness of the space, and furthermore, a tram waits right behind the horse cart stressing the immediacy of the moment. Yet, this is not a modern-versus-primitive vehicle photo, and it does not suggest that the horse cart is old and needs to move out of the way of the more modern tram: the tram will not replace the horse cart. Both are seen as old fashioned. They share the same road or path, and in fact, fate, because they will both be decommissioned in a few years as part of the drive to motorize the streets of the city with new roads and urban renewal.

Just like Cartier-Bresson's, Güler's images were sometimes out of focus, lacking in contrast, distorted in angles, and less determined in composition—the city was a realm of contingencies. Güler was recognized by Cartier-Bresson and his collaborators, and invited to become a member of the famous Magnum (cooperative) photo agency in 1962.[61] The 1950s and 1960s is considered the golden age of photojournalism as a way of story telling; it was partially driven by the magazine market, which declined by the end of the 1960s. *Hayat*, the Turkish equivalent of *Life* magazine, was crucial to Güler's exposure at home and abroad by employing him as staff photographer, and by connecting him to international partners such as *Life* and *Paris Match*.

As many cities began deindustrializing, and as the magazine market and its photographic commissions began declining in the late 1960s and 1970s, inner-city experiences ceased to be a point of attraction for photographers. Istanbul's deindustrialization would start much later, but the local magazine market would also enter a decline in the 1970s. Correspondingly, Güler turned to new interests, such as portraiture. He also started taking pictures in color film, although he remains best known for his earlier work in black-and-white.

PHOTOGRAPHIC MEDIA AND MEMORY

When looking at old black-and-white photographic reproductions of the city's past like Güler's, viewers are transported to a past they did not necessarily experience, or, reciprocally, this other Istanbul moves toward pre-

---

61   Tavlaş (2009), *Foto Muhabiri*.

sent-day viewers and touches them. Black-and-white images act as "melancholy objects," to borrow a phrase from Susan Sontag, who was one of the earliest critics to connect photography to nostalgia, referring to the black-and-white work of Eugène Atget (1857-1927) and Brassaï (Gyula Halász, 1899-1984) in documenting the disappearing "Old Paris."[62] She says,

> Cameras began duplicating the world at that moment when the human landscape started to undergo a vertiginous rate of change: while an untold number of forms of biological and social life are being destroyed in a brief span of time, a device is available to record what is disappearing. The moody, intricately textured Paris of Atget and Brassaï is mostly gone. Like the dead relatives and friends preserved in the family album, whose presence in photographs exorcises some of the anxiety and remorse prompted by their disappearance, so the photographs of neighborhoods now torn down, rural places disfigured and made barren, supply our pocket relation to the past.[63]

This connection to the family album is remarkable. Just as a child who comes to "remember" moments captured in photographs because of viewing and re-viewing the same images in the family album, but may have no other lived memories of the continuum of events leading to and following the shot, certain city photographs come to substitute for actual lived memories. Another thinker to discuss black-and-white as "nostalgia mode" early on in the context of film was Frederic Jameson. Writing in 1984, Jameson defined "nostalgia mode" as a symptom of a crisis in postmodern thought about historical imagination. He explains, "'historicism,' namely the random cannibalization of all the styles of the past" modifies the actually lived past.[64]

In contrast to this negative interpretation of media memories, where nostalgia is equated with forgetting or amnesia, scholars have since pointed

---

62 Emphasis mine. Sontag, Susan (1977), *On Photography*, New York: Picador, pp. 15-16. Later in the chapter entitled "Melancholy Objects," she explains, "Photographs turn the past into an object of tender regard, scrambling moral distinctions and disarming historical judgments by the generalized pathos of looking at time past." (p. 71).
63 Ibid, 16.
64 Jameson (1984), "Postmodernism," pp. 53-92.

out the futility of drawing dualistic boundaries between real and virtual memories, and have begun exploring the relationship between media and memory. Marianne Hirsch coined the word "postmemory" to suggest that the perceived ideal of family photographs can be powerful for both personal and cultural memory.[65] Others have suggested that media and memory are constitutive, or that memories are mostly mediated and in fact, media feeds memory "fever" (hence the intensified desire to record lived experiences through technological reproduction, memorials and museums).[66] In turn, personal or mass media provide layers of memory that the postmodern experimental self can flexibly draw from.[67] Building on Celia Lury's notion of "prosthetic culture," Alison Landsberg has adapted the term "prosthetic memory," to make an optimistic argument that mediated memories can be progressive, allowing individuals to potentially make counterhegemonic readings of mass media representations, and to develop empathy for other peoples' conditions, which may in turn become the basis of new counterpublics.[68]

Güler's photographs of "Old Istanbul" have thus turned into mediated memories through circulation in publications, exhibitions, book covers, as decorative prints in cafes and domestic spaces. Pamuk admits: "I have seen some of Güler's photographs so many times that I now confuse them with my own memories of Istanbul."[69] Yet, this statement is too similar to another the novelist makes in his memoir *Istanbul*, in relationship to old

---

65 Hirsch, Marianne (1997), *Family Frames: Photography, Narrative, and Postmemory*, Cambridge, Mass.: Harvard University Press.
66 Huyssen (1997), *Twilight Memories*. Van Dijck (2007), *Mediated Memories*.
67 Celia Lury argues that a shift is currently underway from aesthetic culture to "prosthetic culture." She believes that a plural society, ordered by variety, is being supplanted by a post-plural society, ordered by diversity. In this new society, the self as possessive individual is being replaced by the experimental self, which requires media representations, especially photographs, for its narration. Celia Lury (1998), *Prosthetic Culture: Photography, Memory, and Identity*, New York: Routledge.
68 Landsberg, Alison (2004), *Prosthetic Memory: The Transformation of American Remembrance in the Age of Mass Culture*, New York: Columbia University Press.
69 Pamuk, Orhan (2009), "Foreword."

black-and-white Turkish films, again from the1950s and 1960s, that are being recycled on private television channels.[70] The circulation of old black-and-white Istanbul pictures, be it photographs or cinema films, in contemporary media provide the "prosthetic memories for imagining "Old Istanbul" since the larger public may not have personal or transmitted lived memories of that Istanbul, and have to rely on technologically reproduced representations such as photographs, films, museums, theme parks, and other simulations to experience it.[71] In both cinematic and photographic works, the recirculation of old black-and-white images of the city reflects an effort to affirm that Istanbul has left behind its provincial, poorer past, has moved on, and that it is ready for its future as a colorful European city.[72] It is also in this sense that the Turkish state, in its various branding agencies, turn to Güler's work to promote Turkey in Europe.

Pamuk is cognizant about the role of black-and-white, and elaborates on it in a layered manner in his *Istanbul* memoir-cum-urban history, in a chapter entitled "Black and White."[73] Here the novelist introduces the notion of seeing the city in black-and-white. He suggests: "[t]o see the city in black-and-white is to see it through the tarnish of history: the patina of what is old and faded and no longer matters to the rest of the world."[74] This mode of seeing metaphorically registers the city's loss of (cultural) color, that is, its former multicultural, multicongressional, and multilinguistic complexity.[75]

Pamuk's is "autobiography as cultural criticism," a genre where the intellectual writes of his earlier life and meshes that with broader interpretations of class, culture, and history.[76] In discussing the novelist's use of

---

70   Pamuk, Orhan (2005), *Istanbul: Memories and the City*, trans. Maureen Freely, New York: Alfred A. Knopf.
71   Landsberg (2004), *Prosthetic Memory*.
72   Fatih Akın's film *Crossing the Bridge: The Sound of Istanbul* (2005) uses the musical scene of Istanbul to argue for the diversity or colorfulness of the city, as discussed by Özlem Köksal in this volume.
73   Pamuk (2005), *Istanbul*.
74   Ibid, p. 38.
75   Ibid, p. 39.
76   Miller, Nancy (1991), "Getting Personal: Autobiography as Cultural Criticism," in *Getting Personal: Feminist Occasions and Other Autobiographical Acts*, New York: Routledge, pp. 1-30. Haverty Rugg, Linda (1997), *Picturing*

photographs in the context of such autobiographies, Gabriel Koureas explains "photography has become a key characteristic of revisionist autobiographies" to help distinguish between different selves, e.g. Orhan in the photograph, Orhan the author—pointing to the role of photography as a prosthesis for the experimental self.[77] Pamuk includes Güler's Istanbul photographs in his memoir (yet does not take issue with their prevalent recirculation and commodification). The memoir is generously illustrated with photographs, many (to my count, 62 of 200) by Güler, the last one being a photograph of Pamuk and Güler in front of a slide table. This collaboration expands into Pamuk's house museum—where the gift shop sells only Pamuk and Güler's work.

While it is palpable how "experimental" subjectivity works in Pamuk's memoir with the aid of photographs, it is less so at a cultural, societal level. Does Güler's work fulfill Landsberg's optimistic argument about prosthetic memories? Do these black-and-white photographs that came to represent a colorful "Old Istanbul" in fact make the city more diverse, or at least open to diversity?

Non-Muslim citizens of the city are, in their absence, central to Istanbul's imagined and marketed societal color. As part of the 2010 European Capital of Culture events in Istanbul, the city's multicultural past was once again on display. Interestingly, to coincide with this year of celebration, Ara Güler published a new book of 56 selected photographs, entitled *Armenian Fishermen at Kumkapı*. It was produced as a single volume in three languages: English, Turkish, and Armenian.[78] The novelty was that the persons in the photographs were identified as Armenian citizens in a fishing community, soon to be displaced by urban renewal. One may argue that this is staged multiculturalism, that the book still does not explore what hap-

---

Ourselves: Photography & Autobiography, Chicago, Ill.: University of Chicago Press.

77 Koureas, Gabriel (2012), "Orhan Pamuk's Melancholic Narrative and Fragmented Photographic Framing—'Istanbul, Memories of a City' (2005)," in *The Photo Book, from Talbot to Ruscha and Beyond*, ed. Patrizia Di Bello, Colette E. Wilson and Shamoon Zamir, London: I.B. Tauris, pp. 211-232.

78 Güler, Ara (2010), *Kumkapı Ermeni Balıkçıları (Armenian fishermen at Kumkapı). Gumgabui hay dzknorsnerě: 1952*, introduced by Murat Belge, Istanbul: Aras.

pened to Armenians or to this particular Armenian fishing community. The photographs and the accompanying essay had originally been published in local Armenian-language newspaper *Jamanak* in 1952 as a six-day series.[79] In contrast, the photographer's prior books such as *Lost Istanbul* and exhibitions on the city had decontextualized the photographs and their original contexts and subjects. The publication of *Armenian Fishermen* does not yet parallel an improvement in the lives of the already-dwindled numbers of non-Muslim citizens in the city today. Yet, it points to a political opening molded very much by nostalgia. Quiet unexpectedly, black-and-whiteness as a nostalgia mode allows media memories of the city to open space for Armenians, and gives viewers (not only the viewers of the book but also readers of its reviews in mainstream print media) the opportunity to develop empathy for the subjects of the photographs.

Güler's black-and-white photographs of "Old Istanbul" have been instrumental in imagining the future of the city as a socially and culturally colorful, open city. The photographer's active curatorial intervention or engagement is key to the limited number of photographs that recirculate from his earlier oeuvre. There is a tension in the reception of the work; by critics and enthusiasts, the work is viewed and consumed as a means of resistance to rampant urban transformation. Yet, by city marketers and governments, it is a picture-perfect depiction of how much the city has improved. Through dissemination in books, exhibitions, and exhibitionary spaces, the photographs have turned into mediated memories of moments viewers may not have necessarily experienced in person. Thus, the photographs have been put to many different uses, including the narration of new selves. What is perhaps not readily recognized is how black-and-whiteness as a representational mode contributes to their reception. In fact, Güler's work has gained meaning in tandem with other exhibitionary sites mediating "Old Istanbul," at the local level and at the transnational level, with the valorization of black-and-white as a nostalgia mode.

* I thank Derya Özkan for inviting me to the conference "Cool Istanbul, Urban Enclosures and Resistances" held at SALT Galata, Istanbul in November 2013, which allowed me to elaborate on what I had previously published on Ara Güler's work in *History of Photography* (2010). I also thank Nancy Micklewright, Head of

---

79   Ibid.

Scholarly Programs and Publications at the Freer and Sackler Galleries at the Smithsonian Museum, for supporting my work and thinking about this subject when inviting me to speak at the Museum, and for coordinating an exhibition about "Ara Güler's Anatolia."

Mirror Mirror on the Wall, Aysel is the Coolest of Them All ...
The Female Protagonist and the Television Series *Kayıp Şehir*

BERRİN YANIKKAYA

> What lives we left behind us
> Not to be lost in the lost city
> Sought shelter in the kindness of this stranger city
> Yet always being strangers in the lost city
> Just like fish hit by the Southwest wind,
> A city slowly sliding into the sea
> Exile is this city, home is this city
> It turns out that there is no other Istanbul
> It's not a fine string, but just a fine twinge
> A love letter from the violin of a lad
> Longing is there, so is reunion
> It turns out that the mirror is here and the key too
> There is no Istanbul other than this one
> There is no Istanbul other than this one [1]

Kayıp Şehir (The Lost City) is a television series that aired on the Turkish national channel Kanal D, between September 14, 2012 and March 25,

---

[1] Sezen Aksu, "Istanbul Yokmuş Bundan Başka," the theme song of the series *Kayıp Şehir* (Lost City). The lyrics were written by Yıldırım Türker, the music was composed and performed by Sezen Aksu. Translated by the author.

Photograph: Derya Özkan

2013. The story was developed by Tomris Giritlioğlu, a well-known woman television and movie producer, and director who often deals with difficult incidents in Turkey's history, such as 1980 military coup and the pogrom of September 6-7, 1955.[2] *Kayıp Şehir* was directed by Cevdet Mercan, the script was written by Yıldırım Türker, Murat Uyurkulak, Seray Şahiner, Hakan Bıçakçı and Leyla Olça, the theme song was composed by Sezen Aksu. Additional music was composed by Demir Demirkan.

Kayıp Şehir can be considered as one of the most extraordinary productions in Turkish television history at several levels. First, the issues that it brought to the public eye had never before been discussed in a popular television drama. Topics such as the ever expanding and interconnected football and parking mafia, and its relationship with politics and the economy, or the collapsed health system and the hope mongers, had never been on public display. Second, the stories of underrepresented and/or misrepresented groups had never been told from their own perspectives in a prime time television series. Third, the locations were chosen realistically, which enabled audiences to witness a layer of the city that is underrepresented in television, along with these people's living conditions. Fourth, the scenes were not prolonged to fit the station's commercial revenue expectations, as opposed to many other popular television series aired on many channels. Therefore, because of its extraordinary characteristics, *Kayıp Şehir* could only survive twenty-six episodes before it was cancelled. The reasons for the cancellation are the very same that attracted the audiences' attention, and are also what make a cohesive analysis of the series difficult. The series was cancelled because it dealt with issues that popular television dramas usually didn't. It was cancelled because of its brave attempt to break the silent agreement to stereotype and bias the portrayal of transsexuals, sex workers, the ethnic and the class-based underdogs of society in a medium intended to entertain people, and sell them to advertisers.

Kayıp Şehir aired on Kanal D beginning September 2012 on Friday evenings. At the beginning, it had the highest ratings. After attracting an

---

2   In the pogrom of September 6-7, 1955, non-Muslim inhabitants of Istanbul were attacked and their property looted by groups of Muslim Turkish people in an act provoked by the state. For more on these events, see Dilek, Güven (2006), *Cumhuriyet Dönemi Azınlık Politikaları ve Stratejileri Bağlamında 6-7 Eylül Olayları*, Istanbul: İletişim Yayınları.

entrenched and loyal audience, it remained one of the five highest rated programs of the evening for a long time. Later, when competitive series started having much better ratings, the channel began to change the show's broadcast day and hour. In the end, Kanal D cancelled the show by claiming that the ratings were not good enough to keep the series in the channel's schedule.

In the following pages, I will try to embed my analysis in theoretical discussions with a particular focus on the character of Aysel. But first, I need to explain how I use the terms script and text when I refer to the written and visual material of analysis. I take the term script to explain how the story is narrated and how the plot evolves through the series. When I refer to the text, I take the television series *Kayıp Şehir* as a whole including its technical, artistic and aesthetic features. Hence, as I analyze the series, although I focus mostly on the text, I also do occasionally address the script in its written and unexecuted form.

The innovative aspect of the series was not limited to the topics it covered. Rather, it was how those topics were narrated. In a city where many people live increasingly isolated lives, without seeing and touching the lives of the urban poor and marginalized populations, *Kayıp Şehir* held a bitter mirror, troubling and at the same time attracting the attention of those who paid no attention whatsoever to people unlike themselves, to the *others* of the city. The series spoke to the conscience of human beings by showing that there are no solely good or bad people. Instead, every person is multilayered and complex. The cultural context the series speaks from is unique in the sense that one must know the historical baggage of the non-Muslim inhabitants of Istanbul, as well as its reflection on collective memory. It is also quite difficult to make sense of the text without knowing the details of Kurdish immigration, widespread male violence against women, unspoken and unseen facts about incest, dominant patriarchal codes, dislocation policies, gentrification sites, and football's importance in popular culture. The plot of the series revolves around the Topbaş family's migration to Istanbul from Trabzon, a city in the Black Sea region, after a flood takes away their home and property. All the other characters' lives interconnect with the family's story throughout the script.

WHAT IS LOST IN *KAYIP ŞEHİR*?

Kayıp Şehir's script was written by the group of intellectuals mentioned above, and deals with issues ranging from the hypocritical moral codes of society to gentrification, the health care system, domestic/internal migration, gender bias, poor working conditions, the corrupt justice system, femicide, solidarity, daily news, mafia, football, ethnic issues and undocumented immigrants, as well as love. In the back streets of Istanbul, in Tarlabaşı, Tophane, and in the back alleys of Beyoğlu, the *others* have been struggling to survive, to endure, to love, to resist, to stay together, to break free, to be a subject, to be the main decision maker of their lives against all odds. Within the *lost city*, Aysel's *otherness* is multilayered. It begins with being a woman, a sex worker, it continues with being madly in love, and ends with becoming a potential home wrecker.

As the protagonist in *Kayıp Şehir*, Aysel is a defiant, broken, tough, wounded, strong, emotional, trustworthy, hurt, fun, sad, lonely, survivor, attractive, moral, fighter, scared, fearless, outspoken, compassionate, flamboyant, subtle, confident, naïve, smart, beautiful and cool woman, indeed coolest of the cool to the core. Aysel is one of the few female protagonists in a Turkish television series depicted with all aspects of her character covered in depth. Indeed, I'd dare to argue that she is *the* female protagonist. In the TV series *Kayıp Şehir*, each and every character takes a stand against being lost or consumed in and by the city. Aysel has been holding her ground for years under the challenging circumstances of urban life, and she seems intent on never giving up.

Most of the female characters in *Kayıp Şehir* are portrayed as much more open-minded than the male characters. For example, the oldest son of the family, İsmail, marries his boss's daughter and they hide in Aysel's flat for a while. Once there, the two women find a way to communicate with each other, and the new wife comes to sympathize with Aysel. Later, when İrfan announces that he will marry Aysel, she supports them, in opposition to her husband's strong objection that Aysel is "morally low." Another example is Seher, the daughter of the family, who talks to Aysel, accepts her as a sister-in-law, and even asks for her help when trying to protect a woman from her abusive husband.

But above all, Aysel is a subversive character that overtly challenges the silent moral agreements of patriarchal social structure. The other female characters act in covert solidarity with Aysel by greeting her, by asking her to join the wedding ceremony, by talking to her. Yet her blunt honesty is bewildering not only to the other characters in the series, but also to the audience. Aysel is a mood changer; she can take the audience up and down with her, switching from crying to laughing or vice versa in an instant. Aysel defies the male gaze for the first time in Turkish television. Her story is told completely from her perspective, by standing at her side, and at the same time avoiding all the clichés about sex workers. She is not someone who has no one, derelict, and she is not abandoned. She is not lonely; she is just alone.

Unsurprisingly, the series ended abruptly after twenty-six episodes during which the show time and date had been changed several times. The series could not run for a complete season. At the time of its cancellation, there remained thirteen episodes yet to be shot. Because of this, loose ends were tied up incongruously with a carnivalesque happy ending. The series served as a mirror that reflected what was happening in the lives of the *others,* and thereby disturbed the value systems of those who did not want to see the other side of the mirror. As such, it is worth going back to the beginning to understand what was reflected in that bitter mirror.

DISCONTINUITY, FRAGMENTATION AND ECLECTICISM
A NEW AFFECTIVE ORDER

The major elements of television series in the era after the 1990s are different from those of previous periods in several respects. Robin Nelson argues that "the new affective order involves a consciousness informed by short but intense sound-vision bytes; non-linearity (in contrast with linear narrative); an information overload; constellatory access to diverse materials; bricolage as its principle of composition; reception- (as much as production-) driven aesthetic; polysemy in respect to meanings; diversity in respect to pleasures."[3] Hence the current style of television series disperses

---

3   Nelson, Robert (2000), "TV Drama: 'Flexi-Narrative' Form and 'a New Affective Order'," in *Mediatized Drama/Dramatized Media*, ed. Eckart Voigts-Virchow, Trier: WVT, pp. 111-118, p. 112, quoted in Allrath, Gaby and Mari-

the audiences' attention in the age where everything from city to narrative, from history to politics and arts, including the subjects themselves, are fragmented. *Kayıp Şehir* holds a distinguished place compared to other television series with its contrasting features in this new affective order. As Casey et. al. point out, this kind of aesthetics favor "modes of thinking and representation which emphasize discontinuity, fragmentation and eclecticism."[4]

There are also other processes involved in the production of television series, such as the specific broadcast policies and schedules of any given television station. Kozloff explains these processes by pointing out that "[t]elevision narratives are unique in the fact that all texts are embedded within the meta-discourse of the station's schedule"[5], that the station "is mainly guided by financial considerations: [S]cheduling has become increasingly important as an aspect of competitive ratings wars".[6] Allrath and Gymnich argue that "[a]s a result of the schedule, TV series, unlike cinematic films, have to fit into largely inflexible time slots."[7] Television stations must place a certain number of commercial breaks and interrupt the series in order to gain advertisement revenue. Yet, in today's world where there are so many other competing entertainment sources, it is not easy to attract audiences' attention. Nelson writes: "[I]n the commercial television industry, the audience must be grabbed in the first forty seconds or it will be lost at the flick of the remote control."[8] Therefore both teasers and open-

---

on Gymnich (2005), *Narrative Strategies in Television Series*, New York: Palgrave Macmillan, p. 4.

4　Casey, Bernadette; Casey, Neil; Calvert, Ben; French, Liam and Justin Lewis (Ed.s) (2002), *Television Studies: The Key Concepts*, London and New York: Routledge, p. 170, quoted in Allrath, Gaby and Marion Gymnich (2005), *Narrative Strategies*, p. 4.

5　Kozloff, Sarah (1992), "Narrative Theory and Television," in *Channels of Discourse, Reassembled: Television and Contemporary Criticism*, ed. Robert C. Allen, London: The University of North Carolina Press, p. 89, quoted in Allrath, Gaby and Marion Gymnich (2005), *Narrative Strategies*, p. 10.

6　Casey *et. al.* (2002), *Television Studies*, p. 204.

7　Gaby Allrath and Marion Gymnich (2005), *Narrative Strategies*, p. 11.

8　Nelson (2000), "TV Drama," p. 113.

ing credits play a crucial role in terms of keeping the audiences in front of the television set for each and every episode of the series.

OPENING CREDITS
ISTANBUL, THE PALIMPSEST CITY

The opening credits of *Kayıp Şehir* run through images of Istanbul. Various parts of the city are depicted with speed shots of over-lighted modern streets and buildings, and slow motion shots of back alleys and rusty buildings. The images are screened one layer over the other, so as to show the palimpsest characteristic of the city. Juan Goytisolo observes that the city is:

[...] a complex semiotic mechanism and generator of culture, [it can] fulfill its mission to the extent that it embodies a fusion of heterogeneous texts and codes, belonging to different languages and levels [...]. The architecture, rites and ceremonies of the metropolis, its layout, the names of its streets and thousands of other vestiges of past epochs appear as coded programs allowing the texts of its history to be constantly produced. The city is a mechanism that perpetually reproduces its own past, and is thus able to confront the present almost synchronically. From this perspective, the city, like culture itself, is a mechanism that opposes time.[9]

Based on this definition, Goytisolo goes on to argue that Istanbul is a palimpsest space in which "new arrivals stand and listen to a polyglot text, babel of languages, language of the stones, tracing the unwritten history of the city founded twenty seven centuries ago according to the promptings of an oracle."[10] The palimpsestic character of Istanbul becomes evident in the sepia-like images that run through the opening credits of *Kayıp Şehir*, accompanied by westernized oriental hybrid music. Whereas the shiny and sterile images of shopping malls and big streets push away the dark, misty and pale images using wipeouts, it is still imminent in the music and in the

---

9   Juan Goytisolo (2003), *Cinema Eden: Essays from the Muslim Mediterranean*, London: Eland Books, p. 71.

10   Ibid., p. 72.

passing images that the city can become whole only by seeing all of its different parts together.

Here we can see an example of what Henri Lefebvre calls the traces of the past right from the beginning: "The past leaves its traces; time has its own script. Yet this space is always, now and formerly, a present space, given as an immediate whole, complete with its associations and connections in their actuality."[11] The dominant visual aspects of the opening credits imply the city, as opposed to the skyscrapers' monumental views and their perceived ahistorical, inhuman, gigantic yet almost unlived appearance. The back alleys are there with their residual stories, human existences, broken yet lived presences. Therefore Istanbul is depicted as a space between memory and loss; remembering and forgetting; ending and never-ending; manufactured and spontaneous; spatial and temporal.

Andreas Huyssen argues that how memory and temporality have invaded media (such as cities, monuments, architecture, and sculpture), which seemed among the most stable and fixed, can be seen as one of the most interesting cultural phenomena of our day. He thinks this shift of understanding has to do with its time: "after the waning of modernist fantasies about *creatio ex nihilo* and of the desire for the purity of new beginnings, we have come to read cities and buildings as palimpsests of space."[12] But the palimpsestic character of a space cannot be interpreted only in terms of spatiality. Huyssen goes on to argue that "an urban imaginary in its temporal reach may well put different things in one place: memories of what there was before, imagined alternatives to what there is. The strong marks of present space merge in the imaginary with traces of the past, erasures, losses, and heterotopias."[13]

---

11 Lefebvre, Henri (2000),"Plan of the Present Work" and "Social Space," in *The City Cultures Reader*, ed. M. Miles, T. Hall and I. Borden, London and New York: Routledge, p. 197.

12 Huyssen, Andreas (2003), *Present Pasts: Urban Palimpsests and the Politics of Memory*, Redwood City: Stanford University Press, pp. 6-7.

13 Ibid. Heterotopia is a term coined by Michel Foucault to describe places and spaces that function in non-hegemonic conditions. He describes how these are spaces of *otherness*, yet they are neither here nor there. He explains heterotopias through their relation to utopias, which have no real place: "There are also [...] places that do exist and that are formed in the very founding of society-

What is said here so far about the traces of the past in the city, can also be applied to literary texts. According to Huyssen "[t]he trope of the palimpsest is inherently literary and tied to writing"[14]. When it comes to the visual representation of urban spaces in cinema and television series, we see that there are more layers added to the already existing ones within the settlement; the camera itself creates another layer. As Orhan Tekelioğlu[15] reminds us, *Kayıp Şehir's* script is successfully inspired by a 1960 movie, Luchino Visconti's *Rocco e i suoi fratelli* (Rocco and His Brothers), and there we see another layer that relies on greeting a classical movie that was set in Milan, the story of an immigrant family from the South, and its disintegration in the industrial North. Altogether, layer-by-layer the palimpsest nature in the text allows the audience to engage with the different layers separately and/or as a whole. Audiences who are able to read the intertextual characteristic of the script can disentangle the knots in the plot through the refined references.

TEXT, MIRROR, WOMEN, MULTILAYEREDNESS

The difficulty in writing about *Kayıp Şehir* originates with the strong contextual references and culturally specific narration, as mentioned previously. The signification of daily life details might make little sense to an outsider, therefore it is not easy to summarize the story of the series in a single sentence or paragraph. Yet the multilayered nature of the text provides

---

which are something like counter-sites, a kind of effectively enacted utopia in which the real sites, all the other real sites that can be found within the culture, are simultaneously represented, contested, and inverted. Places of this kind are outside of all places, even though it may be possible to indicate their location in reality. Because these places are absolutely different from all the sites that they reflect and speak about, I shall call them, by way of contrast to utopias, heterotopias". Foucault, Michel (1986), "Of Other Spaces," in *Diacritics* 16 (1), pp. 22-27, p. 24.

14   Huyssen (2003), *Present Pasts*, pp. 6-7.
15   Tekelioğlu, Orhan, "Kaybolmamak için kayıp şehirde," *Radikal* 2, 7 October 2012, http://www.radikal.com.tr/radikal.aspx?atype=haberyazdir&articleid=1103044 (accessed 16 October 2013).

anyone the pleasure of enjoying a series of stories that can be found anywhere in the world. The plot simply deals with the intersecting lives of people such as undocumented immigrants, abused women, child laborers, ethnic and religious minorities, whose stories remain untold, or framed only in negative ways in popular narratives in mainstream media. In *Kayıp Şehir's* script, their stories are told by constructing multilayered characters in a multilayered narrative through the streets of a multilayered city, Istanbul. This paper analyzes *Kayıp Şehir*, a lost neighborhood television series about the cool city Istanbul, by centralizing the character of Aysel, one of the series' major protagonists. In order to gain insight into the Aysel character, I interviewed Gökçe Bahadır, the actress who played Aysel. My analysis examines the rest of the text through three overlapping concepts, namely *multilayeredness, otherness* and *coolness*. Before elaborating theoretically on these concepts, I need to clarify how these terms will be used in the following pages.

Firstly, I shall give a brief explanation of the mirror metaphor and women's representation in visual media. Anneke Smelik's book *And The Mirror Cracked* (1998) deals with the ways women are represented in film.[16] She points out that "the formal complexity of autobiographical women's films reflects a filmic problem, that is: [according to Elsaesser] how to give the female character in the fiction film a coherent identity, when the very thing that makes her a woman is the constant struggle and failure to cohere."[17] "The issue here is indeed the question of enunciation and the related problems of subjectivity."[18] Smelik discusses the question of subjectivity by giving examples from the German film *The Subjective Factor* (1980) by Helke Sander. In one scene, filmmaker Sander appears on the screen while she watches film footage of herself giving a talk at a student conference thirteen years earlier. Smelik writes: "Within the fictional story, the scene is related to Anni [the filmic character]; both the woman in the present and the one in the past are supposed to be her."[19] Smelik refers to

---

16 Smelik, Anneke (1998), *And the Mirror Cracked: Feminist Cinema and Film Theory*, New York: St. Martin's Press.
17 Elsaesser, Thomas (1989), quoted in Smelik (1998), *And the Mirror Cracked*, p. 40.
18 Ibid.
19 Ibid.

Jochum who claims that "this scene cannot be understood because most spectators would not recognize Sander either in the images of the present or of the past."[20] Yet, Smelik argues that it is not important whether or not audiences actually recognize Sander, since the scene "raises issues of time and history and of authentic versus fictional self: that is, it raises the questions of subjectivity."[21] Smelik claims that "[t]he multilayeredness of subjectivity comes to the fore" in this particular and much discussed scene in Sander's film.[22]

Apart from her analysis of the film, her remarks on changing dominant images and representations of woman and femininity in cinema are worth quoting here. She explains the title of her book based on these changes: "This is how the title of my book, *And The Mirror Cracked*, is to be understood. This study traces the subversive cracks in a mirror, which reflects traditional representations of female subjectivity. When the mirror cracks, splinters also hit the camera eye, introducing if not an actual breakdown in classical forms of representation, at least a shake-up within them."[23] According to Smelik, it is feminism that cracked the mirror, and "once the mirror has cracked, the silver screen will never look the same again."[24] This analysis can be applied to the television screen as well. The medium's own language and economic traits crack the mirror through its tain. Smelik argues that feminism's contribution to this process is not limited to cracking the mirror: "Feminism has undone the mimetic mirror of masculinist culture. Whether by going through the looking glass or by smashing it to pieces, it has made the mirror crack. Feminist cinema has therefore profoundly transformed the traditional field of visual representation, which 'reflected the figure of man at twice its natural size,'[25] while the image of 'Woman' remained diminished and distorted."[26] Therefore, Aysel's multilayered representation is an example of such a crack in the stiff mirror of

---

20 Jochum, Norbert referred by Smelik (1998), *And the Mirror Cracked*.
21 Ibid.
22 Ibid.
23 Ibid, p. 6.
24 Ibid.
25 Woolf, Virginia Woolf (1977), quoted in Smelik (1998), *And the Mirror Cracked*, p. 185.
26 Ibid.

television, which also constructs her as a subject in control of her own life and experience by "[d]iscarding and dismantling old forms of representation."[27] This is why the title of this paper refers to the mirror on the wall. Aysel challenged the traditional representation of woman on television as much as she did the male gaze—a term that I will be addressing in the following pages.

Secondly, I need to clarify what I mean by multilayeredness in terms of explaining Aysel's character in the series as well as the stories of the other characters woven through the text. As Stevi Jackson points out "[e]ven within Western nations the material oppression suffered by women has not gone away, and for many women the situation is worsening as a result of unemployment and cuts in welfare provision. Intersections between class, gender, and racism are clearly important here, too, and need to be pursued in terms of structural patterning of inequality as well as multilayered identities."[28] She feels the need to return to a materialist analysis because materialist perspectives "remain necessary to grapple with the complexities of a postcolonial world, with the intersections of gender, ethnicity, and nationality."[29] According to Jackson, such complexities of the postcolonial world, which are both the consequences and motives behind inequalities, require feminist politics and theory to deal with them through materialist explanations as well as cultural ones.

I will not discuss the materialist approach here in greater detail, yet I would like to emphasize that the culturally constituted differences and postcolonial feminist theories offer useful explanations for my argument. I agree with Ella Shohat and Robert Stam that postcolonial theory "addresses complex, multilayered identities, has proliferated in terms having to do with cultural mixing: religious (syncretism); biological (hybridity); human-genetic (mestizaje); and linguistic (creolization) [...]."[30] Therefore, postcolonial theory's, and especially postcolonial feminist theory's, conceptual-

---

27 Ibid.
28 Jackson, Stevi (1999), "Marxism and Feminism," in *Marxism and Social Science*, ed. Andrew Gamble, David Marsh and Tony Tant, Champaign: University of Illinois Press, p. 33.
29 Ibid.
30 Ella Shohat and Robert Stam (1994), *Unthinking Eurocentrism: Multiculturalism and the Media*, London: Routledge, p. 41.

ization of multilayeredness is important in terms of understanding Aysel's representation, revealed layer after layer throughout the text. In a world where no single nation's borders can limit the implications of social and political change, racial and gendered representations have multilayered, intertextual and heterogeneous characters, as Chandra Talpade Mohanty reminds us, and as Laura Mulvey, bell hooks and Paul Gilroy recognize.[31] The racial and gendered representations, and the social and political implications are rendered through "connections and conflicts between 'cosmos' and 'polis' (city/state), 'cosmos', and the multilayered identity that emerges in a new cosmopolitan era."[32] This new era is marked by the blurred categories that are "unstable, multilayered, incalculable, and [these categories] 'leak,' that is, their meanings spill over into each other and cannot be unambiguously defined."[33] There are no longer any universal meanings that are attributed to concepts of "'the good,' 'the just,' 'the morally correct'" within a postmodern framework.[34] Therefore multilayeredness is rather a complex concept that remains ambiguous and dependent on the contextual references at play in a given situation. At the level of gender representations, this ambiguity is also the result of gender itself being "multilayered in its power effects."[35] The multilayeredness of gender is explained by Selma Sevenhuijsen in the following way:

---

31 Quoted in Meenakshi Durham, Gigi and Douglas M. Kellner (2006), "Introduction to Part IV," in *Media and Cultural Studies: Keyworks*, ed. Gigi Durham and Douglas M. Kellner, Malden and Oxford: Blackwell Publishing, pp. 339-341.

32 Beck, Ulrich (2003), "Rooted Cosmopolitanism: Emerging from a Rivalry of Distinctions," in *Global America? The Cultural Consequences of Globalization*, ed. Ulrich Beck, Natan Sznaider and Rainer Winter, Liverpool: Liverpool University Press, p. 16.

33 Lykke, Nina (2010), *Feminist Studies: A Guide to Intersectional Theory, Methodology and Writing*, New York: Routledge, p. 157.

34 Ibid.

35 Sevenhuijsen, Selma (2004), *Citizenship and the Ethics of Care: Feminist Considerations on Justice, Morality and Politics*, trans. Liz Savage, London and New York: Routledge, p. 48.

Gender works at the *symbolic level,* where images of femininity and masculinity attribute meaning to phenomena which at first sight seem to be separate from it; gender also works at the level of *individual and collective identity,* because the dualisms associated with it control the way in which men and women in our culture develop their self-image, manifest themselves and are judged. It also works on the level of *social structures* because access to (power) resources, social institutions and positions of power are marked by gender norms and gender symbols.[36]

Hence the symbolic level as well as the individual and collective identity, and social structures altogether define the multilayered characteristic of gendered representations. Allrath and Gymnich have a section in their collection under the heading "Multilayered Characters, Multilayered Narratives," in which the authors focus on narrative strategies that undermine coherence in television characters and in unified fictional worlds. In this part of the volume, the chapters by Janine Matthees on *Twin Peaks,* by Klaudia Seibel on *The X-Files* and by Gaby Allrath on *Buffy the Vampire Slayer* and *Angel* deal with multilayeredness in terms of fictional worlds. However, their construction and permeable layers of alternate dimensions[37] show that traditional stereotypical gender representations do not work any longer. In all of the above-mentioned television series, female protagonists are portrayed as powerful, in control, unpredictable and cool in the sense that I will be discussing below.

AYSEL: COOL, WOMAN, OTHER

To understand the new cool female representations in some popular television series in general, and Aysel as the coolest of them all in particular, as I argue in this paper, the elusive concept of coolness must be defined. However, neither grasping a cohesive definition of coolness nor measuring its degree is possible. Hence it would be useful to list the characteristics of coolness instead of trying to define it: Unique, unusual, out of the ordinary,

---

36   Ibid.
37   Allrath and Gymnich (2005), *Narrative Strategies,* p. 39.

aloof, disdain and self-confident;[38] unexpected, surprising, interesting;[39] compelling, temporally and spatially contextual;[40] popular, dynamic, fluid;[41] a style, an attitude, a pose.[42] There is a tendency in contemporary society to name what is cool; it is "a phenomenon that we can recognize when we see it, from its effects in human behavior and cultural artifacts— in speech and dance, films and television shows, books and magazines, music, clothes, paintings, cars, computers or motorcycles. It doesn't take too much investigation to understand that coolness is not something that inheres in these artifacts themselves, but rather in people's attitudes towards them."[43]

Conceptualizing coolness in relation to people's attitudes and/or behaviors is not a new approach; it goes back to ancient times. Nick Southgate argues that Aristotle was the first thinker to introduce coolness in his ethical writings, most particularly in *Nicomachean Ethics*. Aristotle "founded a school of ethical thought known as Virtue Ethics," which meant "that correct behavior is judged in comparison to virtues such as courage, temper-

---

38   Pountain, Dick and David Robins (2000), *Cool Rules: Anatomy of an Attitude*, Clerkenwell, UK: Reaktion Books; J. Schiller, "Who is the coolest of them all," (ACM CHI Workshop on Cool Across Continents, Cultures and Communities, 2012)

39   Gerber, J. P. and Carly Geiman (2012), "Measuring the existence of cool using an extended Social Relations Model," *Psychology Journal* 10 (2), pp. 103-115; Laderman, David (2002), *Exploring the Road Movie: Driving Visions*, Austin: University of Texas Press.

40   Gerber and Geiman (2012), "Measuring the existence of cool;" Pountain and Robins (2000), *Cool Rules*; Schiller (2012), "Who is the coolest of them all."

41   Shriver, Lionel (2003), *We need to Talk About Kevin*. London: Serpent's Tail; Hamermesh, Daniel S. (2011), *Beauty Pays: Why Attractive People Are More Successful*, Princeton, NJ: Princeton University Press; Rentfrow, Peter J. and Samuel D. Gosling (2006), "Message in a ballad: The role of music preferences in interpersonal perception," *Psychological Science* 17, pp. 236-242.

42   Gioia, Ted (2009), *The Birth (and Death) of the Cool*, Golden Colorado: Speck Press; MacAdams, Lewis (2001), *Birth of the Cool. Beat, Bebop, and the American Avant-Garde*, New York: The Free Press.

43   Pountain and Robins (2000), *Cool Rules, p. 18*.

ance, generosity, wit and truthfulness."[44] People pursue happiness in life and they can only be happy when they "exercise each of the virtues in moderation."[45] This approach can be typified as taking an "appropriate response to one's situation. It is this idea of appropriate response that finds rich parallels in the ideas central to the notion of cool. People who are cool are making the most astute decisions about their lives and their environments."[46] There are other references to the historical origins of the term cool[47] yet the link Southgate refers to, here Aristotelian ethics, is particularly interesting to my argument, since it directly addresses people's behaviors.

Within this conceptualization, the rebellion or challenge to anything mediocre, to standard rules and norms of society are parts of the cool attitude. As Southgate points out "It is true that the converse appears to be true of cool's origins as a code of behavior for the marginalized in society. However, like Aristotle, cool is concerned with practical responses to one's situation, e.g. how to react to the day-to-day indignities of oppression with one's (masculine) dignity intact. This practical concern means that cool behavior affects even the minutiae of behavior."[48]

Pountain and Robins argue that one of the misconceptions about coolness is that it is necessarily attached to masculinity. According to the au-

---

44   Southgate, Nick (2003), "Coolhunting with Aristotle," *International Journal of Market Research* 45 (2), pp. 167-189, p. 169.

45   Ibid.

46   Ibid.

47   Southgate (2003). In "Coolhunting with Aristotle" Southgate argues that Aristotle was the first to introduce coolness in his book "Nicomachean Ethics." Pountain and Robbins (2000) and Gioia (2009) argue that coolness was defined in Renaissance Italy by Bardessare Castiglione in his "Book of the Courtier" (1516) where he proposed *sprezzatura* as a way of life, suggesting that we have to cultivate an appearance that allows us to be perceived as performing extremely difficult actions effortlessly. Finally, some suggest that coolness was initially performed by African warriors as a way to appear detached in the face of danger. Pountain and Robbins (2000), *Cool Rules*; Thompson, Robert Ferris (1973), "An Aesthetic of the Cool," *African Art* 7 (1), pp. 41-91; MacAdams (2001), *Birth of the Cool*.

48   Southgate (2003), "Coolhunting," p. 182.

thors, it wouldn't be incorrect to argue that coolness may as well be attached to femininity. It is not a coincidence that women played strong-willed female characters, especially *femme fatale* figures, such as in the film noir genre. Pountain and Robins write:

> It's tempting to see Cool as a primarily male phenomenon, an exaggeration of the young male's tendency toward peacock display and emotional detachment, but it is more complicated than that. There is a sense in which many of the original Cool role models of the '50s—James Dean, Frank Sinatra, Marlon Brando and Montgomery Clift—represented a new feminization of traditional masculine images and a break with orthodox macho constructs of the desirable male. The contribution of gay culture (both underground and 'out') to the development of Cool is a story that has yet to be told. Also in film and popular music there is a long and strong tradition of Cool female role models, from Garbo, Stanwyck, Dietrich and Bacall, through Billie Holiday, to Nico and Chrissie Hynde.[49]

Aysel's coolness becomes visible when looked at from the perspective of Southgate's discussion of cool behavior.[50] In an era when aesthetics trump ethics and politics, Aysel challenges hypocrisy and mirrors the real faces of those who behave hypocritically when faced with her firm character. The ever changing moral judgments of the other characters, especially the males, are highlighted, reminding them and the audiences of her challenging attitude, which is in fact the essence of her coolness. She does not initiate her actions by thinking of the consequences, but on the basis of rightness.

And finally, *otherness* and the *other* must be put into the right perspective so that multilayeredness and coolness can make sense in terms of the *Kayıp Şehir* series and Aysel's positioning within the text. Writing from a postcolonial perspective, Trinh T. Minh-ha claims that *otherness* and marginality became central to theoretical discussions in the 1980s.[51] In these discussions, scholars demanded *the Real Other* to speak the truth about *otherness*. She argues that the *other* is always reminded of his/her *otherness*

---

49 Pountain and Robins (2000), *Cool Rules*, p. 22.
50 Southgate (2003), "Coolhunting."
51 Minh-ha, Trinh T. (1991), *When the Moon Waxes Red: Representation, Gender and Cultural Politics*, New York and London: Routledge.

and is expected to appreciate the opportunity given to speak. Minh-ha writes:

> The game, allowing the *other* an apparent aura, can be very misleading. The fight is always multiple and it needs to be carried out on many fronts at once. Participation never goes without a certain vigilance. What is given in the context of power relations and its systems of dependence is likely to be taken back according to where the wind blows. Flies meet death in sweet honey (Vietnamese proverb). Even and especially when an *other* is being privileged, she is constantly, subtly reminded of the favor she enjoys, and as I have stated elsewhere, of her status as "foreign workers," "migrants," and "permanent sojourners." Moreover, she cannot speak and participate in the production of theories of resistance without bearing in mind she is among those who have been provided with the opportunity to speak her condition.[52]

Minh-ha argues that the *others'* position in society is presented as a privilege assigned to them as long as they remain within the boundaries that have been drawn by *the Master*. The *Master* that she refers to here is the subject in power, he who holds the privilege to define *otherness*. This follows Homi Bhabha's discussion on mimicry and man.[53] Bhabha argues that "colonial mimicry is the desire for a reformed, recognizable *other*, as a subject of difference that is almost the same, but not quite. Which is to say that the discourse of mimicry is constructed around an *ambivalence*; in order to be effective, mimicry must continually produce its slippage, its excess, its difference."[54] For Bhabha, mimicry is "the sign of a double articulation;" it "emerges as the representation of a difference that itself is a process of disavowal."[55] Mimicry, in Bhabha's words, "appropriates" the *other*, and at the same time "visualizes power."[56] Hence the *other's* visibil-

---

52 Ibid, pp. 185-186.
53 Bhabha, Homi (1997), "Of Mimicry and Man: The Ambivalence of Colonial Discourse," in *Tensions of Empire: Colonial Cultures in a Bourgeois World*, ed. Frederick Cooper and Ann Laura Stoler, Berkeley, Los Angeles and London: University of California Press, pp. 152-159.
54 Ibid, p. 153 (Emphasis in the original).
55 Ibid.
56 Ibid.

ity is appropriated by the dominant discourse through a power regime in which the *others* remain within borders silently agreed upon.

Jean-François Staszak points out that there is an asymmetry in power relationships in constructing *otherness*.[57] According to him, power relationships make the dominant group privileged "to impose the value of its particularity (its identity) and to devalue the particularity of *others* (their *otherness*) while imposing corresponding discriminatory measures."[58] Referring to the work of Frantz Fanon and Simon de Beauvoir,[59] Staszak argues that "if the Other of Man is Woman, and if the Other of the White Man is the Black Man, the opposite is not true. Dominated out groups are Others precisely because they are subject to the categories and practices of the dominant group and because they are unable to prescribe their own norms. [...] The power at stake is discursive: it depends on the ability of a discourse to impose its categories."[60]

The discourses that impose the appropriateness of the *others* are mediated through popular media texts as well as the realm of politics. Representation of the *others* in media texts becomes as important as the ways in which discourses around *otherness* are articulated. Minh-ha reminds us of the novelist Zora Neale Hurston's statements about the "Anglo-Saxon's lack of curiosity about the internal lives and emotions"[61] of blacks. As Hurston criticizes publishers' reluctance to print the work of blacks in the United States, she explains their way of thinking by telling a story from American history's slavery period:

---

57 Staszak, Jean-François (2009), "Other/Otherness," in *International Encyclopedia of Human Geography*, ed. Rob Kitchin and Nigel Thrift, Amsterdam and Boston: Elsevier, pp. 43-47.
58 Ibid, 43.
59 Fanon, Frantz (1967 [1963]), *Black Skin, White Masks*, New York City: Grove Press; Beauvoir, Simone de (2010 [1952]), *The Second Sex*, trans. Constance Borde and Sheila Malovany-Chevallier, New York: Alfred A. Knopf.
60 Staszak (2009), "Other/Otherness,", p. 43.
61 Hurston, Zora Neale and Alice Walker (1979), "What White Publishers Won't Print," in *I love myself when I am laughing... and then again when I am looking mean and impressive: A Zora Neale Hurston reader*, Old Westbury, New York: Feminist Press, pp. 169-170.

The visiting master of slaves looked and listened, tried to trap the literate slave in Algebra and Latin, and 'failing' to do so in both, fumed to his neighbor and said: 'Yes, he certainly knows his higher mathematics, and he can read Latin better than many white men I know, but I cannot bring myself to believe that he understands a thing that he is doing. It is all an aping of our culture. All on the outside. You are crazy if you think that it has changed him inside in the least.'[62]

More than sixty years after Hurston's remarks on the Anglo-Saxon perspective towards non-Anglo-Saxon people, similar attitudes by dominant groups towards dominated groups are still present, both implicitly and explicitly through discursive practices. Minh-ha argues that there has been a "move from obnoxious exteriority to obtrusive interiority, the race for the so-called hidden values of a person or a culture, has given rise to a form of legitimized (but unacknowledged as such) voyeurism and subtle arrogance—namely, the pretense to see into or to own the *others'* minds, whose knowledge these *others* cannot, supposedly, have themselves; and the need to define, hence confine, providing them thereby with a standard of self-evaluation on which they necessarily depend."[63] I argue that the voyeurism of the Western gaze and of privileged men in any given society form dominant groups. This manifests itself as the male gaze in visual culture and overlaps at the discursive level with defining women from all walks of life as the multilayered *other:* women of color, ethnic and religious minorities, sex workers, transvestites, transsexuals, gays.

The male gaze therefore becomes a key term in comprehending the multilayered *otherness* of women's representation in media texts. In her 1975 essay, Laura Mulvey[64] describes male gaze as representing women as a spectacle to be looked at. She states that "[t]he presence of woman is an indispensable element of spectacle in normal narrative film," and the woman displayed functions on two levels: at the first level "as erotic object for the characters within the screen story" and at the second level "as erotic object for the spectator within the auditorium," so that the tension shifts

---

62   Ibid.
63   Minh-ha (1991), *When the Moon Waxes Red,* p. 66.
64   Mulvey, Laura (2006),"Visual Pleasure and Narrative Cinema," *in Media and Cultural Studies: Keyworks,* ed. Meenakshi Gigi Durham and Douglas M. Kellner, Malden and Oxford: Blackwell Publishing, pp. 342-352.

"between the looks on either side of the screen."[65] According to Mulvey, mainstream visual culture defines women in terms of sexuality, as an object of desire, as a connotation of to-be-looked-at-ness. Mulvey argues that "mainstream cinema is constructed for a male gaze, catering to male fantasies and pleasures."[66] Uncovering the voyeuristic and fetishistic responses of male spectators to images of women,[67] she explains how the male gaze is constructed in cinema. Mulvey refers to Lacan's "mirror stage" in psychoanalysis, which is "the moment when a child recognizes its own image in the mirror," and which is "crucial for the constitution of the ego."[68] Mulvey connects this observation to a male protagonist's representation in film:

A male movie star's glamorous characteristics are thus not those of the erotic object of the gaze, but those of the more perfect, more complete, more powerful ideal ego conceived in the original moment of recognition in front of the mirror. The character in the story can make things happen and control events better than the subject/spectator, just as the image in the mirror was more in control of motor coordination. [...] The male protagonist is free to command the stage, a stage of spatial illusion in which he articulates the look and creates the action.[69]

Mulvey's discussion about the male gaze suggests that the spectator gains control and possession of the women within diegesis by identifying with the male protagonist in the movie. Challenging the male gaze by using its very own filmic techniques, the television series *Kayıp Şehir* creates a subversive pleasure throughout its text in which Aysel's representation as a sex laborer is never allowed to be exploited by that gaze.

---

65 Ibid, p. 347.
66 Ibid.
67 Chaudhuri, Shohini (2006), "Why Mulvey, Silverman, de Lauretis and Creed?," in *Feminist Film Theorists*, ed. Shohini Chaudhuri, London and New York: Routledge.
68 Mulvey (2006), "Visual Pleasure and Narrative Cinema," *p.* 345.
69 Ibid, pp. 347-348.

FIRST EPISODE: THE ARRIVAL IN THE CITY

To understand the connection Tekelioğlu points to between Visconti's movie and *Kayıp Şehir*, we need to refer to the first episode of the series entitled "Immigration." The first scene involves the arrival of a small town family in Istanbul. As opposed to previous widespread cinematographic depictions of internal migrants from small towns to cities arriving in the urban peripheries and/or ghettos full of fellow villagers, this arrival is into the heart of the city, into a cosmopolitan inner city neighborhood: Tarlabaşı. It is a part of Istanbul with traces of time in space, including the memories of its past non-Muslim populations, with their lived experiences in the 19th century and suffered displacement in the 20th century. As an old truck enters a narrow street, where clotheslines full of laundry span the space between buildings on two sides, members of the immigrating family swarm towards the windows with joy.

As we meet the family members one by one until suppertime, in their faces we see mixed feelings of hope, excitement, and at the same time anxiety for their new life, new beginnings. The oldest of the five sons has been living in Istanbul for some time now. The other family members are a young woman in her early twenties, the mother and the grandfather, who is the father of the deceased father of the children. Their welcome to Istanbul includes chaotic and inexplicable sounds: loud conversations from the street, police sirens, the hustle and bustle in the street, police chasing potential suspects, gun shots, etc. They shut the windows and leave the city outside while Istanbul becomes as small as a two room flat with a football game on television. Soon we find that one of the young men, İrfan is a football player, the oldest son, İsmail is in a relationship but cannot disclose it to the family, the daughter, Seher is a university student, the youngest son Hakan will be beginning primary school, the younger son Sadık is neither a student nor has a profession, and the other young man, Kadir is looking for a job. Money is tight so they'll all have to work. The neighbor who brings some food as a welcome gesture offers to help the mother find a job by saying "this is Istanbul, you cannot not work" referring to the fact that whereas for a woman to work might be seen as an unacceptable behavior in a small town, in Istanbul it becomes a necessity: everybody works to survive.

Meeting Aysel

As the whole family sleeps after the long and tiring day settling in, they wake to a possible intruder's attempt to unlock the door. They all get up and İrfan, the football player, takes a knife before he opens the door. We see a woman, drunk and wasted, with a key in her hand saying "uh f... off, the wrong floor..."

The woman turns to climb the stairs, the mother stops İrfan who makes a move to help her. Then he hides behind the door to listen to the conversation between the woman and a man upstairs. There we hear the cool woman talking, shooing off the man who has been waiting for her. At that moment we sense there is something about this woman, that she will play a central role in the plot. We sense also that there is something unique about her as opposed to her wrecked outlook: she is standing on her own feet, and she is at home with herself. We also sense something else: beyond the televised representation of a call girl, Aysel is the expression of Istanbul with her behavior, with her past and present, with her body, with her resistance, with her coolness, with the layers of her character revealing themselves in time, she is articulated in terms of any and every association there is to be made with the city.

Here we can connect the representation of places with female figures, and the representation of female bodies as palimpsests. Aysel's *otherness* is depicted as multilayered, just like Istanbul, whose each and every level surprises whomever comes into contact with her. In many literary texts and in some semi-theoretical essays,[70] Istanbul is thought of as female. At the connotational level, Istanbul represents all the features that are thought to represent women, and vice versa. Thus, I argue, the imaginary character of Aysel stands for the city of Istanbul, a city that has been mistreated, invaded, unappreciated, incapacitated, sacked, disarrayed and yet still stands with her beauty and all the goodness in her nature, coping with reckless acts of seisin.

Feride Çiçekoğlu's question in her book *The Licensed City* (2007) might bring a different perspective to the symbolic relationship I address here. Çiçekoğlu writes: "[...] the cinematographic images of cities are not only mirror reflections, but also an identity that wanders through the sub-

---

70   Kılıçbay, Mehmet Ali (1993), *Şehirler ve Kentler*, Ankara: Gece Yayınları.

conscious of cities. What can be the representation of Istanbul in cinema?[71] She answers her own question in the following way: "There is an imagery that gives its identity to the cinematographic figure of Istanbul and that imagery is the 'situation of being licensed,' in other words, prostitution."[72] She proposes that the cult movie about Istanbul *Vesikalı Yarim*[73] (My Licensed Lover) connected the image of Istanbul and the protagonist Sabiha's[74] mien. Sabiha's character is a woman who is a sex worker and a mother at the same time, who smokes in the night club yet goes out to the bazaar by covering her hair. Still the most interesting part of her character, according to Çiçekoğlu, is her attitude on advancing upon the city.[75] She argues that "[w]hat makes Sabiha the bearer of modernization in Turkey, is her walk upon us through a male crowd, which makes us her and makes her us in the final scene of the movie. By saying 'us,' I refer to the women who wander around the city alone, who are out at nights, who become integrated with the city without feeling the need of men's guardianship, in short, the women who make the city a metropolis by being present in public space."[76] In this sense, Sabiha in *Vesikalı Yarim* seems to be the prototype of Aysel in *Kayıp Şehir*.

There is also a connection between the representation of places with female figures and the representation of female bodies as palimpsests in western cultures. Gillian Rose argues that the representation of place by female figures can be found in various scales from local communities to nations.[77] I focus on the scale of cities in this sense. According to Rose, "[n]ations have been described as 'imagined communities,' and hegemonic—and therefore idealized—visions of nations also often use female fig-

---

71 Çiçekoğlu, Feride (2007), *Vesikalı Şehir* (The Licensed City), Istanbul: Metis Yayınları, p. 18 (Translation by the author).
72 Ibid.
73 This is a 1968 movie directed by Lütfi Akad.
74 The actress who played Sabiha, Türkan Şoray is given the alias of 'The Sultan of Turkish Cinema.' She started her acting career in the 1960s and took part in more than 200 films.
75 Çiçekoğlu (2007), *Vesikalı Şehir*, p. 19.
76 Ibid.
77 Rose, Gillian (2013), *Feminism and Geography: The Limits of Geographical Knowledge*, Cambridge: Polity Press.

ures to envision themselves; England and France are represented by the allegorical figures of Britannia and Marianne, for example."[78] She notes that "not all places are represented by allegorical female figures;" they

are used only when feminized qualities are being represented.: [...] Man feminized the ideal he sets up before himself as the essential other, because woman is the material representation of alternity; this is why almost all allegories, in language as in pictorial representation, are women.[79]

When it comes to questioning the *other*, Rose argues that "the notion of place itself [...] is that *other*: mysterious, unknowable, beyond language and rationality, and feminine."[80] The female body allegorically stands for the place; hence her body itself becomes the very source of the palimpsest.

When analyzing a novel by Jeanette Winterson, Francesca Maioli reminds us of "how women and their bodies have been too often represented over the centuries in western culture, i.e. as palimpsests."[81] In her analysis of the novel *Written on the Body*, she argues that the "very use of this language as well as the richness of these descriptions and their one-sidedness reminds readers of the metaphysical poets, thus of a male subject gazing at, dismembering and recomposing the fragments of a female, subjugated, body."[82] Maioli points out that in many texts the female body is represented as palimpsest on the one hand, and fragmented and dismembered on the other.

The link between the fragmented and multilayered representation of Istanbul finds itself a surface over Aysel's body, as well as her character. Yet, Aysel is not represented as only the allegory of the palimpsestic city of Istanbul, with all that surrounds her signification in the text (all of her appearance, attitude, experience, defiance, etc.). She is also the subversive female protagonist who challenges the hypocritical moral codes of society,

---

78   Ibid, p. 58.
79   Ibid, p. 59.
80   Ibid, p. 61.
81   Maioli, Francesca (2009), "Palimpsests: The Female Body as a Text in Jeanette Winterson's *Written on the Body*," *European Journal of Women's Studies* 16, p. 143.
82   Ibid, p. 145.

as well as being *the* heroine of a popular cultural text. With her blunt honesty and obvious visibility as a sex worker, Aysel threatens the men's silent agreement with patriarchal and hypocritical moral codes. She is a desirable yet dangerous woman for she does not accept the hypocritical attitude towards sex workers. On the one hand, all the male characters in the series desire her, on the other the moral codes they were raised in demand that they keep away from such an "inferior" woman. This is why they choose to be rude and even violent towards her. In a scene where Kadir warns her to stay away from his brother and family, she looks at him and suddenly discovers that he has feelings for her. She then does not hesitate to say out loud "are you in love with me, man?" The answer comes as a slap in the face. Not being able to face his feelings, Kadir prefers to hurt her both physically and emotionally by insulting her. Here, something unusual happens: she hits him back. She knows the "language of the streets," she knows how to defend herself in a violent environment. Her dignity cannot be taken away from her.

In another scene, the mother of Topbaş family goes after a nightclub's bodyguards when they beat up her younger son Sadık. As the bodyguards are about to become violent with the mother, Aysel sees them by chance. She supports the mother, and puts the bodyguards in their places. The mother, who is the biggest opponent of Aysel's presence in the apartment, appreciates her help. This incident builds a bond between the two women. Hence, Aysel's cool reaction and immediate involvement in the situation alters her reception in the eye of the audience as well. She challenges the repetitive and devaluing representation of sex workers in television.

In many feminist critiques of television, it is argued that television offers a limited repertoire for female roles.[83] For years, women were represented either as "the free, available woman" or "the good wife and selfless mother."[84] In most cases, "television reproduces the ideology of separate

---

83   Brunsdon, Charlotte; D'Acci, Julie and Lynn Spigel (1997), "Introduction," in *Feminist Television Criticism*, ed. Charlotte Brunsdon, Julie D'Acci and Lynn Spigel, Oxford: Clarendon Press, pp. 1-20.

84   Saktanber, Ayşe (1995), "Women in the Media in Turkey: the Free, Available Women or the Good Wife and Selfless Mother," in *Women in Modern Turkish Society*, ed. Şirin Tekeli, New Jersey: Zed Books, pp. 153-169. Once more:

spheres, which sees the home as a space of femininity and leisure and the public world as a place of masculinity and work.[85] The issue of separate spheres is reversed and transgressed by the unconventional representation of Aysel. Aysel is the first heroine featured on television in Turkey that breaks this stereotypical representation of women. This is similar to a representation of Istanbul that would attempt to erase the voyeuristic and/or touristic representation of the city. Many representations of Istanbul are produced by showing stereotypical images, especially when it comes to promoting the city for international sports and cultural events. A similarly reversed and transgressed image can be found in the representation of Aysel in *Kayıp Şehir*.

In cinematographic narratives, the audience's identification with the protagonist is one of the key elements. Yet in the case of *Kayıp Şehir*, according to Gökçe Bahadır,[86] the actress who played Aysel, nobody wants to identify with Aysel. In the interview, Bahadır said she had been told that people wanted to have a friend like Aysel. As such, Aysel's character becomes a subversive element that breaks the identification process. As the actress points out, when she travels around Turkey, nobody wants to talk about her role in *Kayıp Şehir* as Aysel. This is because in the series she plays a sex worker, an "immoral" character, despite the fact that her behavior when dealing with immoral situations in various episodes is morally justifiable, and even admirable.

In the first few episodes, we see that Aysel goes to work. Pressure from television station executives forced a change of plot: she quit sex work and took over a bar with the money she inherited from her late abusive uncle. Although there were no direct references to her work, only suggestions in the dialogue to her profession, as well as in her "immodest" clothing, it became a moral problem that had to be corrected by the television executives.[87]

Feride Çiçekoğlu also talks about this in her book *Vesikalı Şehir* focusing on city/woman.
85 Brunsdon, D'Acci and Spigel (1997), "Introduction," p. 19.
86 The interview with the actress Gökçe Bahadır was carried out in Istanbul, in a coffee house near Bağdat Street, on 11 October 2013.
87 Ibid.

MEETING THE *OTHERS*

As the story unfolds in the following episodes, we see the other *others* and witness their struggles. One way or another, all of their life paths cross with Aysel's. First, the undocumented African immigrant Daniel, who sells perfumes on the streets, surprises the daughter and the younger son of the family when he suddenly appears in the stairwell where he is hiding from the municipal police. Later in the story, he and the daughter Seher fall in love with each other, then he is killed by the police in the street, without due process, and only motivated by Seher's mother's testimony who informs on him to the authorities. The Daniel character is reminiscent of Festus Okey, a real-life undocumented immigrant who was killed in the police station in Istanbul several years ago, as well as of other compulsory immigrants who come to Istanbul on their journey of hope to Europe for a better life. Many cannot make it that far and stay in the *lost city*, trying to be as invisible to the police as possible. After Daniel's death, Seher cannot forgive her mother. She leaves home and becomes an activist. She starts working for a non-governmental organization that helps victims of male violence and women who are in danger of becoming victims of femicide.

A second character that we are introduced to is Duygu, a transsexual sex worker. She is dumped from a car wounded, under a bridge where we see other transsexual sex workers. Aysel takes her to the hospital with the help of İrfan, the football player, who later saves her from being held hostage in the hospital by paying the money for her treatment. Then İrfan lies to her mother saying that he lost the money that was meant to support the family. Yet this philanthropic behavior pays off. Aysel returns the favor by introducing him to Ethem, her ex-boy friend, and owner of a second league football club in Istanbul.

In the end, Ethem becomes jealous of Aysel's relationship with İrfan, breaks his promise to Aysel and does not sign a contract with İrfan, although he plays successfully and scores a goal in a tryout game. Here we see another conventional behavior demolished, when İrfan cries in front of Aysel, talking about his high hopes. And Aysel says "who hits the target at his first try in this city?!" Also Kadir, who will become Aysel's clandestine lover in later episodes, comforts his older brother after this huge disappointment by saying "don't worry, this Istanbul will do us good."

Another group of *others* are the neighbors downstairs. As the plot goes on we understand that they immigrated to Istanbul from the eastern part of the country, that they are one of the many Kurdish families whose villages have been burnt down. Zehra, the daughter of the Kurdish family is also Kadir's co-worker, and would later become first his fiancé and then his wife. Her father, a truck driver who is usually away, loses his job and tries to cope with the pressures of traditional values. He suffers as a man who cannot support his family. At this point, the script deals with two issues at the same time: the dislocation of a so-called ethnic minority and the feudal codes that are coerced and encoded into being a "true man."

A historical mesh is drawn from the story of the silent grandfather of the family. He goes on pursuing a woman he met years ago. Later, we understand that he took part in the pogrom of September 6-7, 1955, in which non-Muslim property was attacked and pillaged. As such, the plot attempts to reckon with a dark era in the city's past, in this case, violent acts against the non-Muslim inhabitants of Istanbul.

Another group of *others* are called *apaçi*s. This subcultural group consists of young men from the peripheries of the city. They wear distinctive hairstyles and use a specific dress code. Sadık, the younger son of the family first gets into trouble with them and then they become friends. *Apaçi*s try to help a sick friend whose mother also works as a sex worker. To help, they make money by getting involved in illegal activities ranging from a car park mafia to stealing a truck full of groceries. In this part, the series deals with health care problems, and how the urban poor suffer from a highly privatized health system. Another related problem is touched upon with the conman who gives false hopes to the sick boy's friends by claiming their friend can walk again after a surgery.

Ethem, Aysel's ex-lover, keeps pushing Aysel around and wants her to be with him again. He also has a lot of connections with underground businessmen, and has a web of shop owners paying him illicit tributes. At the same time, he is married with a child who is named after Aysel. The double life of some rich and powerful businessmen in the country is brought to the attention of audiences in this character. Ethem has a twisted moral code when it comes to anything to do with Aysel. He gets jealous of İrfan and kidnaps her. During the period when Aysel is held captive, there is a scene which I believe will be remembered in Turkey's television history for many years. Aysel and the guards sit in the barn and play poker. That scene shows us another part of Aysel's multilayered character; she is able to cope with any kind of situation in her very own way, and she definitely is a survivor. The dialogue in this scene convince us of Aysel's many years of experience dealing with tough men in the streets.

Towards the end of the series, we are introduced to another major social problem in Turkey, femicide. The social organization where Seher works gets a call from a woman who is in need of immediate protection from her husband. They give her a room to stay with her daughter Çilem in the non-governmental organization's office.[88] However, after a while, the husband locates the organization's building and one night when Seher and the woman are alone in the building, he attempts to break in. They then try to find another temporary place for the woman to stay. Seher asks Aysel whether or not she would be able to host the woman and the child. After seeing Çilem, Aysel takes them in and İrfan gives them his full support and promises to protect them. The solidarity amongst women is presented through the things they do at home together; cleaning, singing, and cooking. At that moment, the doorbell rings, the mother goes to open the door, and Aysel and the little girl hear a single gunshot. The husband who has followed Seher from the organization's building found his wife and shot her dead at the door.

The murder of the little girl's mother forces Aysel to make a decision about whether she should keep her or call social services. İrfan suggests that although their relationship did not work, they can become Çilem's parents and give her the life she could not have under state protection. Aysel buys a ring and proposes to İrfan. After letting Çilem change her name to Peri,[89] İrfan introduces her to his family as a granddaughter. For the first time, he defies his mother and declares that he and Aysel are going to get married.

The oldest son-İsmail's wife support him as does Seher, his sister. Yet the strongest and most unexpected support comes from the grandfather, who celebrates his grandson and welcomes Peri to the family. Aysel breaks several unwritten rules by adopting the child of a femicide victim, proposing to İrfan, and accepting to become a member of a highly traditional family from the provinces. Yet, by so doing, she gives up on her love and

---

88 Çilem can be translated into English as "my suffering."
89 Peri can be translated into English as "pixie."

becomes her lover's sister-in-law. By this point, Kadir has decided to sail away with a long-distance commercial boat with support from his wife Zehra.

Kayıp Şehir attempted to help the *others* in society become visible by sidelining the narrative along Istanbul's past and present stories. All there is and was in the city could be found revealed in the plot, layer after layer. It is an aestheticized yet realistic counter-hegemonic text. As opposed to an elitist modernism,[90] *Kayıp Şehir* tried to depict the *others* with genuine lives in Istanbul. As with any other bitter mirror, it was face down, with the *others* invisible in the representations of the city on the big twisted Mirror called television.

---

90 Günebakan, Deniz, "Kayıp Şehrin Ardından," *Biamag Cumartesi*, 29 March 2013 (http://bianet.org/biamag/toplum/145471-kayip-sehrin-ardindan, accessed 16 October 2013).

Index

accessible 22, 68
advertising, advertisement 27, 42, 51, 58, 70, 110, 118, 136
aerial 90, 96-98
aesthetic, aesthetics 7, 8, 21, 24, 28, 36-37, 39, 40, 42-43, 52, 58, 89, 118, 133-134, 136, 146-147
aestheticization, aestheticized 16, 161
affirmative, affirming, affirmation 13-14, 32, 35, 38
Akın, Fatih 8, 81-82, 90, 126
anger 55, 74
anthropology of space and work 71
Africa, African 24-26, 29, 44, 58, 101, 146, 158
African-American 26, 27, 29
Alfama 86-89, 101
ambivalence 89, 148
apaçi 159
Armenian 104, 116, 127, 128
artistic production 8, 36, 44, 50
Atget, Eugène 119, 124
authentic, authenticity 17, 83, 141

authority, authoritarianism 14, 48-49, 70, 158

barricades 59
bebop 27
becoming 19-20, 30
belle époque 112
belly dancing, belly dancer 14, 16, 17
black-and-white 8, 94, 103-105, 111, 116-119, 123-124, 126-128
Black Atlantic 24
Black Culture, Black American culture 27, 58
Black Sea 133
blue collar 8, 63, 69, 73
biennal 20, 52-55
Birmingham School of Cultural Studies 42
body, bodies 8, 25-26, 30-31, 46, 65-67, 71, 74, 153-155
Bosporus 31, 90-92, 94, 95, 98
brand, brands, branding 21, 40-43, 52-53, 58, 65, 69, 70, 78, 114, 126

Brassaï 124
bridge 8, 31, 81-83, 85, 90-96, 98-101

call center 61-62, 65-67, 71, 73
Cartier-Bresson, Henri 119, 123
city marketing 21-22, 114
colonial, colonialist 16, 48, 86, 114
commodity 38-45, 52, 70-71, 78
commodification 16, 43, 85, 101, 127
common, commons, common wealth 15, 21, 46, 56, 111
confinement 73, 74
construction 62, 65-69, 71-72, 74-77, 96, 100, 111, 144
consumer 27, 40-41, 65, 77, 83
consumption 22, 28, 41, 53-54, 57-58, 106
coolhunting 46-47
cool Istanbul 7-8, 13-17, 20, 22, 25-26, 31-32, 62-64, 69-70, 77, 81, 128
coolness 7-9, 15-16, 19-21, 23-27, 29, 31-32, 38, 41, 54, 63, 82, 140, 144-147, 153
cosmopolitan 15, 106, 108, 113, 116, 143, 152
creative 31-32, 43-45, 50, 55-57, 70-71
cuisine 17
cultural capital 26
cultural diversity 91
cultural field 47
culture industry, global culture industry, culture industries 7, 35, 40-41, 50-52, 55-56, 58-59, 70, 78
cultural memory 125
cultural production 16, 19-21, 40-41, 43, 50, 56, 78

decentralization 70
desire 21-22, 29, 57, 85, 87, 101, 114, 125, 138, 148, 151, 156
difference 7, 15-16, 18, 21, 40-41, 45, 47, 50-51, 53
dignity, dignified 23-24, 26, 77, 146, 156
disciplining of labor 68, 71
dissent 20, 28
distinction 29-30, 48, 68, 72, 74, 114, 119, 124
diversity 15, 18, 66, 91, 93, 104, 125-127, 135
dolmuş 100
domination 75
dream, dreams, dreamy 65, 71-72, 75, 82, 86, 88, 117

economic capital 76
emotional 29, 68, 134, 147, 156
enclosure 21, 23, 31, 62, 77, 81, 128
enlightenment 40, 47
entrepreneurial city governance 106
Erdoğan, Yılmaz 96
Erfahrung (Walter Benjamin) 68
Erlebnis (Walter Benjamin) 68
European Cultural Capital 81, 84, 85

event   40, 52-58, 84, 99, 124, 127, 132, 151, 157
everyday   13, 21-23, 27, 32, 35, 37, 39, 52, 54, 57, 71, 107, 118-119
exchange   7, 19, 38, 40, 42-44, 46-47, 49-50, 56-57, 64, 78
exclusion, exclusionary   16, 78
expectation engineering   67
exploit, exploitation   15-16, 22, 58, 75, 151

factory, factories   39, 54, 62, 64-65, 68-69, 71, 74-75, 77
fado   83, 86-87
female   8- 9, 18, 96, 134, 144, 147, 153-156
femicide   134, 158, 160
feminine, femininity   141, 144, 147, 155, 157,
feminist   8, 141-142, 156
feminized   14, 155
femme fatale   147
flexibility, flexibilitization   18, 68, 76
football   132-134, 152-153, 158
foundation university   61, 66-68, 70, 74
fragmentation, fragmented   62, 72, 136, 155
Frankfurt School   48, 70
Freiburg School   48-49

gecekondu chic   16
gentrification   15, 56, 78, 133-134
gerontocracy   75
Gezi   22, 31-32, 55-58, 76, 115

global economy   83, 100
government, governmentality   8, 15-16, 20, 26, 45-46, 48, 50, 54-55, 70, 106, 115-116, 128
Greek   112
Güler, Ara   8, 94, 104-123, 125-129

habitus   30
Hayat   123
health   27, 63, 69, 73, 76-77, 132, 134, 159
hegemony, hegemonic, counter-hegemonic, non-hegemonic   9, 16, 19, 38, 44, 48, 54, 56, 125, 138, 161
heterotopias, heterotopic   138
hierarchization   72
Hine, Lewis   108, 119
hip, hipster   14, 27
hüzün   87, 93
hybridity   14, 142
hypocrisy, hypocritical   134, 147, 155-156

imagination, imaginations   7-9, 13-20, 24, 31, 55, 70, 77, 82, 88, 98-101, 124
immaterial   16, 22, 30, 32
imperfection   18, 20
in-between, in-betweenness   101
inclusion, inclusiveness   15-16, 110
inequality, inequalities   50, 54-55, 69, 73, 142
informal   16, 18
insurance   61, 65-68, 71, 72, 77

Istanbul Biennial 20, 53-55
Istanbul Eats 17

jazz 17, 26-27, 54, 59, 78

Kayıp Şehir/Lost City 8, 131-134, 136-137, 139-140, 147, 151-152, 154, 157, 161
kebab 17
kırmızılı kadın (woman in red) 58
Kurdish, Kurds 21, 91, 93, 133, 159

labor 3, 8, 39, 42-45, 47, 50, 55-56, 62-64, 66-68, 70-71, 73-77, 105, 119, 140, 151
laboring bodies 66-67
laboring worlds 66
laissez faire 49
leisure 39, 157
liberal, liberalism 45-50, 57
lifestyle 41, 52
loss 86-89, 92-93, 106, 126, 138
liberation, liberating 25-26, 28-29, 32
Life 123
lieux de mémoire (Pierre Nora) 112

Madredeus (band) 83, 85-86
Magic Carpet Ride 96-98
Magnum (photo agency) 111, 119, 123
mainstream 20-21, 28, 30-31, 57, 59, 67, 77, 91, 115-116, 128, 140, 151

male 14, 29, 96, 133-135, 142, 147, 150, 151, 154-156, 158
male gaze 135, 142, 150-151
manual labor 64, 67
market, marketing 8, 21-22, 37-41, 43-53, 65, 67, 74, 78, 83-84, 92-93, 97-98, 106, 114, 116, 123, 127-128, 146
masculine, masculinity 14, 75, 144, 146
material 15-19, 22, 30-32, 42, 64-65, 135, 142, 155
meaning, meanings 24, 26, 30, 32, 35-36, 38-39, 41-42, 50, 58-59, 89-91, 99, 101, 108, 117, 128, 135, 143-144
media memories 103, 124, 128
melancholia 93
memory 86, 88, 94, 103, 111, 122, 125, 133, 138
Men on the Bridge 96, 100
mental labor 67-68
migrant, migration 17-18, 21, 74, 78, 106, 108, 112, 119, 133-134, 139-140, 148, 152
mimicry (Homi Bhabha) 148
mirror stage (Jacques Lacan) 151
misuse 13-14
monochrome, monochromatic 8, 111, 117-118
multicultural 81, 90, 116, 126-127
multi-ethnic 106
multilayered 8, 46, 133-134, 139-144, 147, 150, 153-154, 160
multi-religious 106, 109
multitude 22, 31
mystification 26

myth   44, 86-87, 99

Nar Photos   115
neoliberal, neoliberalism   8, 15, 22,
    34, 36, 50, 57, 112
Newsweek   14-15, 19, 22, 25, 32,
    35
non-conformism, non-conformist
    23, 25, 28
non-governmental organization,
    NGO   67-68, 71, 107, 158, 160
non-Muslim   18, 108, 113, 116,
    127-128, 132-133, 152, 159
normative   7, 13-14, 36-37, 77
nostalgia, nostalgic   8, 82, 86-89,
    90, 92-94, 98-99, 101, 104-106,
    108, 110, 113-114, 118-119,
    124, 128

Okey, Festus   158
Old Istanbul   104, 110-111, 113-
    114, 116, 118, 125-128
Old Paris   119, 124
oriental city   14-16
others, otherness   9, 133-135, 138,
    140, 147-150, 153, 158-159,
    161
outsourcing   73, 77
Özge, Aslı   19, 96, 100

palimpsest   137-139, 153-155
Pamuk, Orhan   87, 92-93, 114,
    125-127
Paris Match   123
periphery, peripheries   39, 78, 152,
    159
plaza   62, 65-66, 68, 70, 74

pogrom of September 6-7, 1955
    132, 159
political economy   7, 18, 23, 42, 51
popular culture, popular cultural
    26, 30, 36, 39, 42, 133, 156
popular media   8, 149
popular television   132, 144
post-colonial   142, 147, 148
post-fordism, post-fordist   7, 15-
    16, 18-21, 26, 28, 34, 39-40,
    45-46, 50, 53-55, 57
postmemory   125
precarious, precarity, precariat   54-
    56, 58-59, 73, 75
producer   13, 58, 65, 132
production of space   7, 14
productive labor   39
project management   66
proletarianization   45, 72
prosthetic memory   125
prostitution   154
psychodynamics of working life
    63

rapid urbanization   108
rehabilitate, rehabilitating   22
repression, repressive   23, 26, 29,
    32, 56
resistance   20, 22-23, 26-27, 30-32,
    43-44, 55-59, 62
resources   15-16, 21, 25, 45, 52,
    54-55, 144
Riis, Jacob   108, 119-121
risk   20-21
Rocco e i suoi fratelli (Rocco and
    His Brothers)   139

Saudade 87
script 85, 132-34, 138-140, 159
self-confidence 20, 25
self-fashioning 20, 26
service 53, 55, 64, 67, 70-71, 77, 160
sexuality 14, 75, 151
sex work 9, 132, 134-135, 150, 154, 156-159
slave trade 24, 26
social capital 70
social ontology 20, 26
social reproduction 39-42, 44, 47, 72
solidarity 74-75, 77-78, 134-135, 160
souffrance au travail 63, 73
sovereignty 16
spontaneous, spontaneity 18, 77, 138
stereotypes, stereotypical 7, 14, 16, 92, 144, 157
Stieglitz, Alfred 122
stratification 74
street art 18, 21
street photography, street photographer 94, 119-120
subaltern 38, 42
subcontract, subcontracting, subcontractor 72, 76-77
subculture, subcultural 35, 38, 159
sublime, sublimity 7, 21, 30, 32, 37-42, 44, 52-53
subject, subjectivity 8, 14, 16, 18, 20, 23, 26, 28-30, 40, 44, 46, 50, 58, 62-64, 92, 121, 127,
134, 140-142, 148-149, 151, 155
success 21, 47, 54, 56, 71, 84-85, 90, 94, 158
Sulukule 18
symbolic capital 69-70

Taksim 70, 72, 74, 76, 105, 115
Tarlabaşı 18, 21, 134, 152
technological reproduction 97, 111, 117, 123, 125
third world city 14-16
tourist, tourists, touristic, tourism 31, 55, 62, 81, 84-86, 88, 92, 113-114, 157
transsexual 92, 132-133, 136, 144, 150, 153, 158

Unique 37, 77, 85-87, 89-90, 92
unqualified 72-73
urban 14-16, 24, 35-36, 53-56, 62, 64-65, 68-69, 74, 76, 78, 81, 97, 106, 108, 112-113, 119, 123, 126-128, 133-134, 138-132, 152, 159
urban cultural common 21
urban enclosure 62, 77, 81, 128
urban poverty 16, 18, 108
urban transformation 15, 18, 21, 36, 76, 128
use value 38, 40-42, 78

Valorization 8, 107, 113, 118, 128
value, valuable, values 35-44, 47, 52-53, 55, 57, 58, 66-68, 72, 78, 135, 149-150, 159
Vesikalı Yarim (movie) 154

Visconti, Luchino 139, 152
visual culture 93, 150-151

Well-being 69
Wenders, Wim 81-89, 92
white collar 8, 63, 67-70, 74
work 8-9, 18, 27, 32, 45, 47, 51, 55-57, 59, 61-78, 100, 103-106, 108-120, 123-128, 132, 134-135, 148-150, 152, 154, 156-160
working class 55, 64-65, 108-109
work misery, work miseries 63-64, 71, 73-75
work of art 37, 38, 42-45, 52
workplace 62, 64-66, 68, 71-76
workspace 64-65, 74
world cinema 81-83, 90
world music 82-84

List of Authors

Özlem Köksal received her Ph.D. degree from University of London, Birkbeck College in 2011 with a dissertation examining the relation between collective memory, history and cinema in Turkey. She has published various articles and reviews both in English and in Turkish and she is the editor of *World Film Locations: Istanbul* (Intellect Publishing, 2012).

Aslı Odman is a Ph.D. candidate at Bosphorus University, Istanbul and works as an Instructor in the Department of Urban and Regional Planning at Mimar Sinan Fine Arts University, Istanbul. She works on the concretization of labor practices and capital accumulation processes in urban spaces, in other words on "the production of space through human agency," with a special historical focus on the interwar period. She currently does anthropological research in various labor geographies of Istanbul focusing on working people's health and precarity.

Aras Özgün is a media studies scholar and a media artist. He earned his Ph.D. degree in Sociology from the New School for Social Research, New York. He produces experimental media works and writes in scholarly journals on media, culture and politics. He is currently teaching at the Cinema and Digital Media Department of İzmir Economy University, Izmir, and at the Department of Media Studies and Film at the New School for Public Engagement, New York.

Derya Özkan received her Ph.D. degree in Visual and Cultural Studies from the University of Rochester in 2008, completing a dissertation titled "The Misuse Value of Space: Spatial Practices and the Production of Space in Istanbul." She joined the Institute of European Ethnology at Ludwig Maximilian University of Munich as a Postdoctoral Researcher in 2008. Since November 2011, she has been holding a DFG Emmy Noether Fellowship and leading the Research Group "Changing Imaginations of Istanbul. From Oriental to the 'Cool' City." Her research interests are situated at the intersection points of urban studies, visual studies, cultural studies and migration studies.

İpek Türeli is Assistant Professor of Architecture at McGill University, Montreal. Her research focuses on visual culture, comparative urbanism and architectural history. She is the co-editor of *Orienting Istanbul: Cultural Capital of Europe?* (with Deniz Göktürk and Levent Soysal, Routledge, 2010; translated, revised and printed in Turkish as *Istanbul Nereye?* Metis, 2011), a book that explores how processes of creative production and exhibition are intertwined with neoliberal urban restructuring in Istanbul.

Berrin Yanıkkaya received her Ph.D. degree from the Sociology and Methodology Doctoral Program, Institute of Social Sciences, Mimar Sinan Fine Arts University, Istanbul. She became an Associate Professor in Communication Sciences in 2010, and has been working at the Department of Radio, Television and Cinema, School of Communications, Yeditepe University, Istanbul since 1997.